REVISIONS

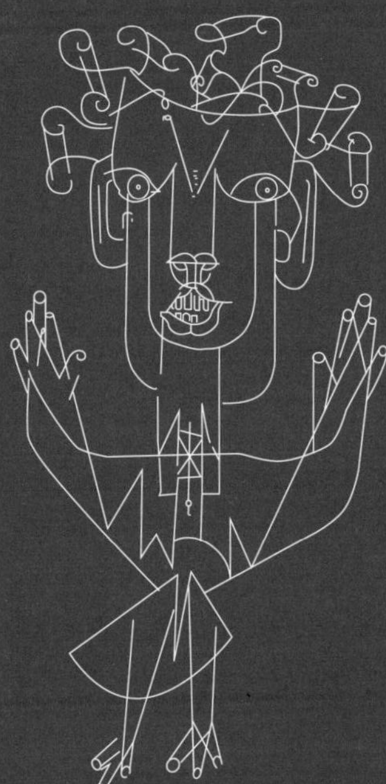

REVISIONS
Yvonne Rainer
Essays by Apollo Musagète, Yvonne Rainer, and Others
Published by no place press

Edited by Rachel Churner
Contributions by Gregg Bordowitz, Emily Coates, Douglas Crimp, and Anna Staniczenko

ISBN: 978-1-949484-05-2

English
Printed in China

Cover: line drawing after Paul Klee, *Angelus Novus*, 1920.
Designed by Geoff Kaplan/General Working Group
Distributed by The MIT Press

no place press
New York and San Francisco
noplacepress.com

REVISIONS

Essays by Apollo Musagète, Yvonne Rainer, and Others

YVONNE RAINER

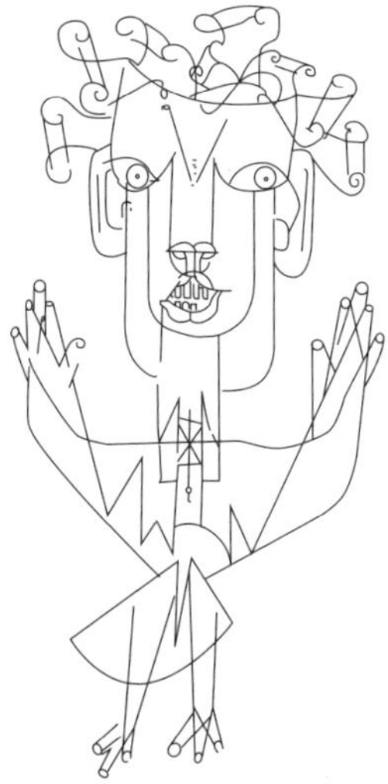

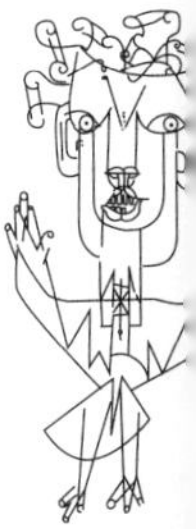

Everything Under the Sun (for YR)
Gregg Bordowitz

> . . . your funny side is very often overlooked. Your work is often seen as overly intellectual, maybe because you're known as the theoretician of Judson, and because in your films you often took on serious political topics—class privilege, rape, cancer, racism, the battle of the sexes. People focus more on the pedagogy and less on the vaudeville.
>
> —*Douglas Crimp to Yvonne Rainer*[1]

Yvonne Rainer's methods of composition are remarkably consistent across multiple mediums, including choreography, performance, film, writing, and teaching. The methods require:

an acute awareness of the present;

a rule of measure to cast the immediate past into phrases or passages;

a cut-and-paste procedure for combining these passages into sequences;

the ability to juxtapose these sequences, employing the qualities of gravity, weight, velocity, and duration so that each quality takes its own form according to the medium in question (dance or writing, movements or words).

Gravity in a dance is often quite literally understood. It is emphasized through the choreography of dancers' bodies, their movements often drawn to the floor. Objects, like chairs and pillows, are used both as support and falling matter. In written texts, gravity is taken as a metaphor. The topics, the tone, the repetition of words, all are measures of gravity on the page.

The same can be said for weight. A body landing on a stage is different from a sentence laid out on a page, yet both communicate weight.

Velocity is a matter of acceleration or deceleration, though feet in dance travel differently than foot in prosody.

Duration is largely a subjective quality; each viewer can experience an hour of clock time as fleeting, and a short moment as interminable. In YR's work, duration is most often determined as a matter of exhaustion for the artist, the dancer, the performer, the audience, or the reader. This is not a criticism. It's a fact. YR's compositions aim toward exhaustion.

Or maybe exhaustion isn't the right word. The compositions are exhaustive. They so thoroughly consider every permutation and angle within the constraints and limits of every situation, context, and medium in which they appear.

Read this book as an instructional manual, paying attention not only to the contents of the page but to the composition of the text. "Pedagogical Vaudeville 3" is an example of a process explained to others in a form that embodies the very process itself. This text includes a compilation of emails sent from YR to the teachers and students of a school where Rainer will conduct a workshop resulting in a production. The very composition of the text possesses all the qualities of the method described above within the constraints of a particular device, email.

Our email boxes are a repository, at once a camera, a voice recorder, and the combined minds of the participants. In this text, YR uses emails like the pages of Sigmund Freud's "mystic writing pad," the analyst's notes marking the slips and lapses of the analysand/writer/composer. YR's procedures are forms of self-analysis with the single self multiplied into a manifold subject by one abiding proposition.

YR's pieces are always an undefeatable logical proposition. Any particular work "is and is not" a list, a transcription, and a copy of a copy of a copy, ad infinitum toward a point of exhaustion. Maybe exhaustion IS the right word! YR's works exhaust. They are examples of spontaneous combustion. The artist and all involved burn-out to burn up. Fire isn't the only element that comes to mind. Burning cold, like dry ice that passes from solid to gas, bypassing liquidity. They are liquidations. All this wordplay is necessary to describe what exists at the center of YR's conundrums. What does the work mean? Everything and nothing.

All five texts in this manual serve the same purpose to both describe and become the working processes of its author. This includes Anna Staniczenko's essay "Challenging the Canonical: Yvonne Rainer's *AG Indexical with a Little Help from H.M.*" Staniczenko's writing is an important contribution and commentary on YR's methods. The essay clearly, thoroughly, and accessibly details the ways that YR's dance *AG Indexical* is and is not a copy of a copy of a copy of George Balanchine's *Agon*. Staniczenko understands and demonstrates how YR absorbed the lessons of Balanchine and her predecessors into an ablation.

An ablation is:

> the surgical removal of body tissue;
>
> the removal of snow and ice by melting or evaporation, typically from a glacier or iceberg;
>
> the erosion of rock, typically by wind action;
>
> the loss of surface material from a spacecraft or meteorite through evaporation or melting caused by friction with the atmosphere.

The analogy to ablation is mine, not Staniczenko's. Still, Staniczenko's research in combination with YR's texts testify to a transformational event that calls to mind a chemical transformation of elements.

Or did I mean to say chimerical? Chimera (in Greek mythology) is a fire-breathing female monster with a lion's head, a goat's body, and a serpent's tale; or it is any mythical animal with parts taken from various animals. A chimera is also a thing that is hoped or wished for but in fact is illusory or impossible to achieve. Certainly, YR's script—"Revisions: A Truncated History of the Universe for Dummies / A Rant Dance, Lecture, and Letter to Humanity by Apollo Musagète (with notes by Yvonne Rainer)"—is chimerical. It's a work of mythology in which the ancient Greek god Apollo inhabits the body of Yvonne Rainer in the form of the avatar Apollo Musagète. Bigendered, ageless, and timeless, the god Apollo, his avatar, and YR simultaneously manifest in one convergence to persuade humanity to right its evil ways. Like Freud, YR marshals Greek mythology to explore the unconscious. Instead of the Oedipus myth, YR becomes Apollo associated with music, poetic inspiration, archery, prophecy, medicine, pastoral life, and significantly with the sun. Apollo is the sun god, but not just any one. He's the Greek God. The names of all the sun gods of the ancient world are too numerous to mention here including Aztec, African, Arabian, Chinese, Semitic, etc. That YR chooses Apollo shows that her unconscious still arrogantly revolves around Western mythology (implicating many in the audience).

To further complicate matters, YR or Apollo peppers their tirade with Yiddish phrases. Is the sun god a New York Jewish intellectual?! Perhaps, YR has in mind Kohelet, the Hebrew biblical author of an ancient book known to most by the Greek title Ecclesiastes. Ecclesiastes is considered somewhat of an anomaly in the Jewish Bible. It is essentially a piece of Stoic philosophy with some incongruous imperatives to follow God's law spliced-in so that the text appears to be religious instruction. Kohelet's message is simple: all is vanity, there's nothing new under the sun, achievement, wealth, petty grievances, we all share the same fate (death), and the best you can do is moderately enjoy food, drink, and bodily pleasure. Kohelet is not a hedonist. And he's not Apollo.

Yet, Apollo is the one to appear as a chimera, and he is pissed! Apollo cares deeply about the human fate and he bitterly complains, visits judgments, and describes in excruciating detail all his godly efforts to keep the sunrise on schedule as he inveighs against dictators, politicians, celebrities, and everyday people — Come to your senses! Get the world spinning aright! Or more correctly left, as Apollo is apparently a Democrat leaning to the socialist side.

More, I can't tell you. Read this book. Read it more than once because nothing is as it appears and everything is significant.

1. "Yvonne Rainer Interviewed by Douglas Crimp, October 4, 2012," in this volume, p. 91.

Revisions: A Truncated History of the Universe for Dummies
A Rant Dance, Lecture, and Letter to Humanity

by Apollo Musagète (with notes by Yvonne Rainer)

September 23, 2017

To Whom It May Concern:
My name is Apollo Musagète, Leader of the Muses, God of the Sun. Just so you won't worry about who's minding the store up there while I'm away, let me reassure you that Calliope and Melpomene have taken over my job of guiding a sun chariot across the heavens every day. The truth of the matter is that I came down to Earth this time around for a well-deserved vacation, but also at the invitation of choreographer Emily Coates, who was about to present her work about Balanchine and his ballet *Apollo* in New York City. She asked me to play myself, rather than Yvonne Rainer, in the piece. It was an offer I couldn't refuse.

Emily must have heard of a performance of mine that took place some fifty years ago at Judson Memorial Church at a time when I was trying my hand at choreography. I had invited Isaac Newton to be my partner in an erotic duet, during which fifty red rubber balls were to be thrown down one at a time from the choir loft of the church. He declined. He objected to my choice of fifty rubber balls rather than a single Gravenstein apple, but also said I was too old for him. I had to admit that I'd been around quite a bit longer than he had! Anyway, Emily's dance received a good review in the New York Times. (Uh, by the way, mine didn't.) So you see, your Earth is not an entirely unfamiliar place to me.

There was another performance that Emily may have attended years ago, titled "Forti, Paxton, Rainer Read Their Writings." (Be aware, this time I was embodying Yvonne Rainer, who is a little hard of hearing and sometimes slow on the uptake, as you shall soon see!) The three of us read from our writings in ten-minute increments three times. On his third turn, Paxton forgot to give a signal at the end for the projection of a film of a very peculiar and colorful spider, so when his light faded as he made his exit and my light came up, there was confusion as to what had happened. I just assumed that he had decided not to show the film, but when I saw Forti get up from her position and go over to talk to him, I left mine to ask her what was happening, and I thought she said, "He forgot to bring the film." I then returned to my position and started to read. But when I had finished, I began to seethe, "Why hadn't he told us before the show? (Why didn't I figure out that he had simply forgotten to give the cue for the projection? No, I continued to be pissed.) But then, lo and behold, the spider film was projected! I said to myself, "What the fuck!" and went over to Steve and said as much. Of course, he didn't understand why I was so upset. During the bows, I (still embodying YR) punched Steve in the shoulder, to which he responded, "Fuck you!" and I replied, "Fuck you too!" (I wonder if during the applause any spectators were able to lip-read that exchange!)

[I must confess that from my Apollonian perspective, I still don't see why I should be held accountable for Ms. Rainer's dim-wittedness.]

I really do miss dancing, however. I've been thinking of a solo; I even have a title: "Swan Song and Last Hurrah." It has lots of swearing and complaining about the state of your world and the lousy shape it's — and I am — in, but I guess it will have to wait.

At this point, before immersing you in a more expanded account of my earthly escapades, and at the risk of taxing your patience, I must describe a recent mundane, though traumatic, event that took place almost as soon as I arrived in order to dispel any further illusions you may have of me as an invulnerable superior being. From past experience I should have known that a god does not impersonate a human being without a certain amount of risk and that my hasty embodiment of Yvonne Rainer this time around may have been ill advised. In hindsight, I would have fared better if I had given myself more time to look around. But I digress . . .

So that I might prepare myself for at least one of the ways in which middle-class mortals in industrialized countries conduct their lives, I visited a northern-Manhattan gymnasium with the intention of spending half an hour on a recumbent bicycle. Because someone was already occupying that machine, I decided to try the treadmill. So there I was, trudging along at a fairly brisk pace, when for some unfathomable reason I pushed a button that caused the damn thing to instantly take off at fifty miles an hour, catapulting my feet behind and landing me flat on my back on the floor in shock and at a loss as to what had happened. The end result was deep abrasions on both legs — I have the scars to prove it! — and considerable humiliation witnessed by, fortunately, only one other person who happened to be in the room.

On top of the above pratfall, the front doorknob where I was staying fell off; one of Yvonne Rainer's hearing aids, along with her reduced-fare MTA card, bit the dust; and the apartment became infested with bedbugs.

The following week I moved out and did a lot of lying around in another friend's digs, feeling sorry for myself while watching sitcoms and appalling international news reports and wolfing down shitloads of comfort food and wondering if these experiences were typical of life on Earth in the postmodern era.

During this time I also saw an unsettling movie on TV: *The Shop on Main Street*, made in 1965, about a small Slovak village during World War II that had come under Nazi control. The main character is a hard-drinking carpenter. Though lacking sophistication and any particular ideology, the carpenter is hostile to his overbearing, Nazified brother-in-law, who, as an enabler of the occupiers' Aryanization plans, has authorized him to take over a sewing notions shop owned by a somewhat senile and deaf Jewish woman. The Jewish community then offers the carpenter a weekly payment if he takes over the store, which would otherwise be given to a new, possibly ruthless Nazi sympathizer. The old lady accepts him as someone who will be helping her take care of the shop, and she welcomes his daily presence.

I had been familiar with some of the grosser details of the Holocaust and its victims. For instance, in a conversation with the Italian writer Primo Levi some years before he committed suicide, he described a bizarre incident that took place in Auschwitz: a guard casually wiped his dirty hands on Levi's prison jacket, as though he were nothing but a towel at another human's disposal.

The banality of evil came surging back to me while watching the various characters in this film play out their complicity and passivity as the Nazis began to round up the Jews in the town and appropriate their means of livelihood. The carpenter drinks more and more as he witnesses the tightening noose and tries at first to persuade the confused shopkeeper to hide. When she finally realizes what is happening and in horror utters the word "pogrom," the game is over. He knows that it is either his life or hers that is at stake and tries to push her out of the shop into the organized awfulness taking place in the town square. I won't describe the dénouement. The film stayed with me for days, and I was so distressed at being reminded of that time and place in European history that I vowed never to go there again, during this or subsequent earthly visits.

(I cherish a far more touching and unexpected experience when, during prehistoric times, I watched some grieving Neanderthals throw bouquets of flowers into the graves of their departed. To think that I had to contend with the incredulity of your anthropologists when I described this custom! You so-called moderns should stop using the "Neanderthal" label as an insult when the evidence clearly shows that Neanderthals displayed sensitivities and intelligence equal to your own.)

It seems like decades, maybe millennia, before my hapless Rainer pratfall — I'm not the only god who loses track of time — that I was drafted by Zeus (a.k.a. Jupiter) to come down here to get things straightened out for youse guys. In one of those early efforts I approached that capricious voyager, Ulysses (a.k.a. Odysseus). I had made a special trip out to his ship to appeal to him. "Ulysses," I said, "Stop farting around with Scylla and Charybdis and get yourself home to Penelope. She doesn't know whether you're alive or dead and is just about to give up on you. Go home, Ulysses. Go home!"

And did he listen to me? No, he did not. Unfazed by my Apollonian authority, he had himself tied to the mast so he could listen to those ladies singing off-key out on that island. I guess you gotta do what you gotta do.

Around the same time there was Ariadne, who — no, sorry, it was **Eurydice** who died from a snakebite and landed in the Underworld. Her boyfriend Orpheus had asked me to go down there to help him negotiate a deal with Pluto (a.k.a. Hades), who was so charmed by his lyre-playing that he agreed to let her go, but on one condition. On the way back, with Eurydice following us, I was filled with trepidation and felt compelled to remind him: "Orpheus, you were warned not to look back. She's right behind us. No need to look back at her. Puh-leeze don't look back!" Well, we all know what happened to HER — and him, eventually. (I have to confess I still feel a little guilty about her. Would he have turned to look if I had kept my mouth shut?)

Then there was that heel, Achilles. I tried to reason with him. "Look, man, you've been at this heroics game long enough. Let Hector find someone else to punch in the nose. Take a rest. You've made your mark on the world. Isn't it about time you retired?" And gimme a break with that Trojan horse, Homer! I couldn't believe how anyone could be so gullible as to bring that thing into the city. Even after I joined forces with the wailing Cassandra, it was pointless to try to stop them. In every instance — Ulysses, Achilles, Homer, the Trojans, everyone! — it was like talking to a wall.

Which reminds me: Pay no attention to those unsubstantiated rumors that I raped Cassandra and was the cause of Daphne's being turned into a tree. The truth about Cassandra and me is that we had a brief consensual affair, but then she complained to her mother that I had seduced her with books, that I had made her read all of Proust, Tolstoy, and Dostoevsky in rapid succession, which in her eyes was as good as telling her she could order her wedding dress![1] Needless to say, at that point I made one of my many hasty exits.

I admit I've said and done some shameful things in my day, like forcing sex on my Muses and allowing two of my suffering cats to live too long before having them euthanized. I could describe many more instances of objectionable behavior, guilt for which has impelled me to return to Earth from time to time for a shot at redemption. From my present vantage point, however, and with enduring admiration for Cassandra for her activism during the Trojan War, let me assure you that, all in all, I'm not such a bastard as I used to be, as you shall see for yourselves soon enough as I proceed.

Now that I'm here in what you call the twenty-first century, I plan to visit all the temples dedicated to me, and beyond that, I also see it as a duty to lay more of that stern advice on you mortals. So last week I decided to kill two birds with one or two stones, first visiting the Temple of Nabo Apulo in Palmyra, then going on to Damascus for an audience with Bashar al-Assad, the president of Syria. Both excursions were disappointing. Big-time. The temple was a shambles and Assad turned out to be a real scumbag. If anyone needs reasoning with, it's **him**. I went over there and got my foot in the door. (Needless to say, I was very polite.) "Mr. Assad," I yelled through the partly open door. "Mr. Assad, with all due respect, what kind of country do you think you're going to rule when all this is over? The entire population will be either dead or fled. Why, I couldn't even get near the gates of Aleppo, so many refugees were streaming out" ("thick as thieves," I refrained from adding).

He slammed the door in my face, nearly breaking my foot. The same thing had happened with Agamemnon in Mycenae after I berated him for going to war over a single broad. And that idiot King Lear, who couldn't see what was in front of his nose. I told William if he couldn't do better than that, I wouldn't show up for his coming-out party. And then there was OEDIPUS! I pleaded with Oedipus not to kill that old guy in the road. I knew if he did that all hell would break loose, especially after that weirdo in Vienna got so stuck on him. Once again, my entreaties were to no avail.

After many centuries of such rebuffs I was getting pretty demoralized. Mind you, I've approached countless more troublemakers who subsequently disdained my proposals, like that overachiever Charlemagne and your current badasses: Duterte in the Philippines, Modi in India, and Rump in the United States for starters, shameless demagogues flaunting their calculated venalities. Their policies and machinations trap the majority of their citizens in the vast gap between a glossy democratic ideal and a squalid undemocratic reality. As a consequence, your human masses have long stored up feelings of injury, inadequacy, and envy and are predisposed to believe in more nonsense than any other species on Earth. No rabbit, for instance, would have been willing to crash an airplane into the World Trade Center in the expectation of being rewarded with 72 virgin rabbits in the afterlife![2]

In every instance my interventions were rejected. And furthermore — and much to my chagrin — I couldn't even begin to pique anyone's interest in the difference between transcription, transcendence, and analogy, which in my mind was as momentous an area of research as theories of gravity and acceleration, space/time, and Einstein's General Theory of Relativity. *Oy,* one failure after another.

So I decided to go back to my shrink. I told Dr. Kellerman the whole story. Without missing a beat, he responded, "Apollo, you're barking up the wrong tree. How can you expect them to pay attention to you when you're running around down here like a mere mortal or a chicken with its head cut off? Where are your twelve black stallions and golden chariot? Get them out of storage. You've got to make a grand entrance. Only then will they take you seriously."

"Are you suggesting I should make a spectacle of myself?" I asked.

"Absolutely," he replied. "Go for it!"

I went out of there thinking, "This guy is well worth his two hundred bucks an hour." I hurried back to Olympus and started to clean up my golden chariot. And whaddya know? Obama called. Yes, ***THAT*** Obama, Barack. "You've got to come down here. Hillary needs you!" He sounded stressed.

"I'm coming. I'm coming!" I assured him. And I quickly finished polishing my golden chariot and hitched up the twelve black stallions. After persuading Calliope and Melpomene to traverse the heavens every day in my absence in a somewhat shabby carriage, the only replacement I could muster at short notice, to be drawn by a team of sturdy mules, I set out for Earth.

Oy veh ist mir! Alas and alack! I had totally forgotten about the pull of Earth's gravitational field. We got burnt to a crisp, and I was reduced to a subatomic particle of cosmic dust. Who would listen to me now?!

It wasn't easy, but I persevered, and, after looking in vain for a phone booth, finally got through to Hillary on a borrowed iPhone. I asked her, "Why don't you fly out to Michigan or Wisconsin and listen to those people? Many of them have legitimate grievances. They can't find jobs, and they're sick and tired of being abandoned, betrayed, ignored, and condescended to by the likes of you. Granted, some of them may harbor a deep-seated racism in addition to their class resentments, but they can't all be neo-Nazis and misogynists. You can't just call them derogatory names. What is it you called them? Rhymes with 'adorable.'"

For added emphasis, I quoted novelist Édouard Louis, who, while discussing the indignities of poverty, said in an interview, "When you are subjected to endless violence in every situation, in every moment of your life, you end up reproducing it against others in other situations, by other means."[2a]

Which only partly explains the outcome of the U.S. presidential election in 2016. Long before voters went to the polls, I felt strongly that Hillary needed to be reminded of the loathsomeness of the numbskull she was up against, or, as someone called him, a fucking moron, and another, even better, an enigma wrapped inside a whoopee cushion.[3] I did manage to warn her, "If you don't reach out and make eye contact with those people, before you know it they'll go for the first loudmouth schmuck that comes down the pike."[4]

And guess what she said to me? She said, "I don't know what you're talking about." (Had she never heard Yiddish before?) In spite of her tone-deafness, I can't say I disliked her. Under the current circumstances, however, and although it's pretty clear the cards were stacked against her from the get-go — the shenanigans of the Electoral College, for instance, probably sealed her fate! — I can't help thinking that it's time for her and her regrettable husband to retreat into the shadows. They've had their day in the limelight and have nothing more to offer.

At this point it would be remiss of me to assert that over the eons we on Olympus have not made comparable and irrevocable mistakes, especially with respect to women. Always underestimating them, always blaming them for every evil that ever beset humankind. When Zeus created Pandora, for instance, it did not have to be a foregone conclusion that she would open that box, thus releasing untold miseries upon the world. I saw it coming but didn't put my foot down strongly enough. I was too diplomatic. I should have cautioned him, "Zeus, are you sure you want to handle her in this manner?" I should have suggested that he insert a waiver that would have legally prevented her from opening the box or at least have given her a choice. After all — and in my estimation, things have changed only incrementally — if women aren't invited to the table, they end up on the menu. I've always regretted my timidity regarding the Pandora calamity.

So what is to be done? I mean, right here and now, on Earth! I've had to recoup, re-strategize. William Faulkner said somewhere, "The past is never dead; it's not even past." And *I* would add, "Sometimes it rises up and grabs you by the throat." On the heels of the Hillary debacle, this does not mean that you should judge the failures of progressives and idealists of the past by the abhorrent acts of the present. Both occur at different moments of struggle. These days I tell every mortal I meet: No need to set your hair on fire. You're in this together. You are not alone. You are not powerless. Be resilient; you will get through this. Be patient, not reckless. As one journalist wrote, "The brick, the bottle, the fist, the fire: Fierce resistance by the oppressed makes for a better story than the drudgery and temporizing of lawmaking and coalition building."[5]

Yes, all the more reason to ORGANIZE! Make alliances. History doesn't always advance; it sometimes stalls, even regresses. "Freedom and liberation are an unending task."[5a]

And to offset my qualified call to arms, allow me to end with a favorite quote from the late Amiri Baraka: "What can I say? It is better to have loved and lost than to have put linoleum on your living room floor."[6]

Sorry, I can't stop. As Leto, my mother, used to say when she had had a bad night's sleep, "My mind kept working." My mind these days is prey to an endless loop of atrocities. Today I'm stuck in 1916 during World War I. A young soldier is running along the edge of a trench, one arm missing, bleeding to death, knowing he is done for. Yesterday I was somewhere in the Middle East. Two men were carrying another man's inert body, his penis stuffed into his mouth. And the day before that I found myself on a beach in Turkey as the corpse of a small child washed up. Much earlier, in 16th-century Cuba, I had to turn my eyes away as the conquistador Cortés hacked off a young woman's arms when she protested the burning of her sweetheart. And in 1792 I attended the first public execution by guillotine in Paris.[7] The crowd was dissatisfied. They felt the guillotine was too swift and clinically effective to provide proper entertainment, as compared to previous execution methods, such as hanging, death by sword or ax, or breaking at the wheel. The public even called out, "Bring back our wooden gallows!"

Punishment was a spectacle then, and if you were a criminal, your body was doubly violated: first executed (in public) and then chopped up on the anatomist's slab. Execution was corporeal revenge: torture, death, and dismemberment, sometimes not even in that order. There were stories of still-breathing bodies being dissected. Anatomy specimens were scarce, and the scarcer the specimens, the higher the price on the black market and the lesser the criminal charge punishable by a death sentence.[7a] In general, the treatment of the poor was hardly better than that of alleged criminals. Your forebears were undaunted by practices that, by today's standards, one would think are taboo; and yet, in one month, according to a recent New York Times article, 542 Syrian civilians were tortured to death by the Assad regime.[7b] And if anything could be worse, I was witness to the horrendous spectacle of hundreds of Syrian villagers being felled by sarin-gas attacks by the criminal Assad's air force. First they bomb the hospitals and then they drop the nerve-gas bombs, so much more effective than the theatrics of the 18th century.[7c]

Even when *reading* about such atrocities in the New York Times, I get stopped in my tracks; for instance, by a report about one of the first U.S. interventions in Afghanistan in 2010: "The engineers left the helicopter first, hauling explosives. One of them would be dead by noon."[7d]

I need an aspirin or something to alleviate the torment of all these images etched on my brain. Polyhymnia, one of my favorite Muses, keeps nagging me, "Apollo, leave the foul planet before Zeus gets a headache and sends a meteorite, as he did to that town in Siberia in 2013. Those guys were lucky then; they may not be again, and then who'll have the headache?"

"Not yet, not yet," I keep telling her. "They've got me by the short hairs. I have to believe I can still make a difference down here." Maybe I can get to the bottom of things through more fieldwork. There are so many unanswered questions, such as: "Was there a single moment, relatively speaking, in the history of the world when homo sapiens first took a wrong turn?" Artist/adventurer Renée Green had an interesting take on this question in a recent exhibition: "Humans fight and lose the battle, and the thing that they fought for comes about in spite of defeat, and when it comes it turns out not to be what they meant, and other humans have to fight for what they meant under another name."[8]

And this leads to yet another dilemma: Why did Western historians become so invested in the notion of progress in the face of overwhelming evidence that it could so readily collapse into domination, vengeance, and amnesia? When I broached this question over pizza and beer with my old chum Walter Benjamin shortly before he landed in the Underworld, he had this to say: "The idea of a universe with infinite repetitions, without any finality or goal, was a counterpoint to the Enlightenment's faith in progress." Notice that he used the word "counterpoint" and not "rejection" or "refutation." An even more critical view of the Enlightenment states that "'Reason' became another name for bourgeois oppression, the triumph of science merely an excuse for more orderly forms of social subjugation."[8a] Obviously, I have more reading to do. Let's hope that the results will pay off for you mortals.

While I was still roaming around Earth, looking for answers and trying to help out, there was a solar eclipse across the U.S. in the summer of 2017. Calliope and Melpomene were dismissive of all the excitement down here. Earth's moon poses little threat to us Olympians. And your Earth is four hundred times larger and more powerful than your barren satellite. Yet I found myself far more attentive to this event than I had been thirteen hundred years earlier, when Earthlings thought a solar eclipse augured the end of the world. My interest this time around can be attributed to all the fancy gadgets you people have since developed for solar measurements. The eighth century had nothing to compare with the devices common in the twenty-first, such as telescopes, thermometers, particle accelerators, barometers, spectrometers, pyranometers, coronagraphs, and all manner of gauges and scopes like balloons and airplanes and roosters, all of which livened things up during your recent eclipse. (OK, maybe I've overstated. The 8th century probably had roosters, whose cock-a-doodle-doing calmed people's hysteria as the Sun reappeared.)

During the previous summer, as a passenger on a cruise ship that was sailing around the Outer Hebrides, I was making small talk — incognito, of course — and telling a fellow passenger about a woman who had risen to prominence advocating for women's rights in a Middle Eastern country. After she was captured by Islamic State militants, they taped her mouth shut and strung her up with her wrists bound behind her back and her feet dangling two inches from the ground. Before I could finish the story, my shipmate asked, "Are you interested in history?" Not wanting to show my hand, I was somewhat evasive. I could have talked up my ideas about choreography and politics and making something out of nothing, which would have led to how the critics had vilified me years ago and all but drove me out of the dance world back to Olympus. One of them derisively wrote, "He walks as though he's in the street!" and another: "Someday there will be a real murder in one of his dances." As though my aversion to stylization and illusionism was tantamount to criminality! On a bad day their words still rankle. But here on this laid-back cruise I was not inclined to indulge such spleen for these convivial vacationers, so I cut the conversation short with "I am one of those artists who makes beauty out of misery."

My cruise mates were nursing shots of Laphroaig on the upper deck while I surreptitiously imbibed nips of ambrosia from my hip flask. The evening Sun — less resplendent than when I was last in charge but still navigated by Calliope and Melpomene — broke through the dappled clouds and bathed our faces in a beatific glow. My innards, unaccustomed to mortals' gourmet cuisine, complained of abuse. My shipmates were pleasure-seekers, not the dispossessed; amnesiacs, not the oppressed. They wore Issey Miyake, not . . . They were like the lotus-eaters, their sleep untroubled. They laughed and laughed, and didn't weep. They were deserving, had paid their dues, worked for their money, suffered along the way, put in their time. They had no reason to deprive themselves or scrimp, flinch, flagellate, bemoan. They agreed the world was going to hell in a handbasket, but "dear God," as one of them remarked, "allow us this rollicking reprieve, a moment of relief on the woeful planet."

The skipper opined, "It's coming, not in my lifetime, but some day we will find a way to leave the Earth behind." "But some of you will have to stay," I thought, "the unlucky ones and, without a doubt, the impoverished ones." It wasn't the first time I held my tongue.

Eventually, as the ship was putting into port, there — lo and behold — standing on the dock was Terpsichore, all aflame and very pissed off. "Zeus sent me down," she exploded. "His message is, 'You've accomplished next to nothing down here. Shit or get off the pot!'" She raced on, wouldn't let me get a word in edgewise. "Calliope and Melpomene are fed up with driving that cheesy chariot and those stubborn mules across the heavens every day, and I'll be damned if I'm going to help Hercules clean out the Augean stables every morning for your fucking precious idle black stallions! You're shirking your responsibilities. Wind up your affairs down here and get your ass back to Olympus. Zeus is getting heartburn." She fumed on and on. I was able to placate her at last by offering a trade-off. I was willing to bring two of her favorite choreographers, Trisha Brown[9] and Nancy Meehan,[10] back from the dead if she would intercede with Zeus to allow me to stay here a little longer. She hesitated, then made a counteroffer: "Throw Ian White[11] into the mix and I'll take it up with Zeus." I had barely nodded my head in agreement before she was gone.

Without waiting for Zeus's go-ahead, I set out for the Underworld to retrieve Nancy, who I felt was a more likely candidate, as she had arrived there most recently. This time Charon had raised his price for ferrying people across the River Styx. Turning my pockets inside out, I managed to scrape up enough cash to cover a one-way trip and shortly reached the far shore and the entrance to the gloomy home of the dead. Much to my surprise, Cerberus, the three-headed canine guardian of the gate, gave me no trouble. After talking Pluto into offering the same contract that Orpheus had signed for the ill-fated Eurydice, I took Nancy by the hand and we fled from that place. Confident of a more felicitous outcome, we began the long, steep climb toward the light at the end of the tunnel.

Speaking of entrances and exits, at this point I would like to take a slight detour in order to contrast how gods and humans come into the world and some of you depart from it. For all the talk about the origins of the gods, like Athena emerging from the head of Zeus, your own means of earthly arrival is, for reasons I've never understood, a taboo subject on Olympus. My guess is that Olympians are repelled by the messy manner in which humans are born: the bursting of that membranous bag of amniotic fluid, the final plop of the ejected placenta, the clinging umbilical cord that must be severed, the newborn covered in bacteria, if not shit or, technically speaking, meconium. Luckily, we on Olympus don't have to contend with any of that. I have been told that in the past a blare of trumpets announced the arrival of the gods at the beginning of time, but there has never been even a trace of primordial ooze to accompany it, nor any sign of those icky semen-encased entities called spermatozoa that helped put all of you in motion!

But make no mistake, there *are* some downsides to being a god: Coming into existence fully formed as speaking adults, we never experience unconditional parental love and childhood wonderment, and then on top of that early shortfall we must cope with the chronic fatigue of immortality. Despite such drawbacks I would be most unwilling to trade them for your untidy beginnings and obsessive deferrals of ultimate demise by way of those ubiquitous treadmills and spin classes, to be shortly followed by everlasting nothingness and red roses laid on your graves, the latter signaling a more fragrant and tragic exit for some of you than your start in life.[12]

Now taking a pendulum swing in another direction, allow me to describe a recent trip to El Paso, Texas, at the southwestern U.S. border with Mexico, where I witnessed infants being torn from the arms of parents who had come north to escape marauding gang violence in Central America. Knowing what you know of Olympians, you're probably aware that children have never loomed large in our lives. Nonetheless, I was caught completely off-guard by the extremity of my feelings at the sight of those inconsolable and traumatized kids. Wonder of wonders, imagine an Olympian experiencing human empathy, as if I had suddenly recovered a long-repressed memory of a similar trauma. Maybe I've been down here too long; I need this kind of thing like a hole in the head — so much misery on this planet, but your repellent moron's treatment of these CHILDREN is an example of exceptional callousness.

No, I'm not getting sentimental, although I must admit that listening to Pablo Casals playing Bach on his big fiddle can make me well up, and a few days ago, as I stood in front of a 1950 Clyfford Still at your Metropolitan Museum in New York City, I started to cry. Be that as it may, I didn't applaud the cynical asshole when he reluctantly signed an executive order calling for the cancellation of his immigrant child/parent separation policy, all the while suggesting he was being "weak" for doing so. I can't believe this guy — it would have been nice if either his wife or daughter had warned him that he would lose his base and jeopardize his cronies' success in the midterm elections if he didn't sign. But, of course, his base is totally impervious to, but rather applauds, his every abuse of power.

In the midst of these reflections I received a letter from artist Monica Majoli, who wrote:

> The utter helplessness of these people. The Holocaust comes to mind. The destruction of records, which would reunite them, the lucrative deals for those erecting detention centers (of course all roads lead to money in our country — especially now). It's a sickening feeling, beyond language. Maybe that's why after 18 months of unspeakable, relentless, multifaceted violence to justice, democracy, ethics, civility, precedent, humanity, progress — our capacity to reflect the magnitude of it in words fails us.

Majoli's citing of the Holocaust reminds me that the Nazis, evil as they were, kept meticulous records and knew what they were doing, unlike the bumbling neophytes who have replaced the more seasoned civil servants at every level in the U.S. government. Your numbskull's tactics around the immigration situation are as staggering a display of mendacity and stupidity as his Helsinki debacle,[13] both of which should have surprised no one.

It has only recently occurred to me that the president of the United States has no center. Neither duplicity nor incipient dementia can entirely account for this; it's more likely an extreme and unacknowledged amorality that keeps his toadies and victims alike in a state of perpetual anxiety and instability. His lies parade in front of a fundamental narcissism that sustains his obliviousness to the devastating effects of his tweets and edicts with their distractions, distortions, and misinformation. According to a recent poll, almost a quarter of the Republican electorate think that Rump should close down mainstream news outlets like CNN, the Washington Post, and the New York Times.[13a] One columnist wrote: "Spectacle is his métier. He's indisputably spectacular. And even if it's a ghastly spectacle and presented that way, it still lets him control the narrative."[13b] I can't help thinking that he's less an aberration or anomaly than a symptom, and even when he himself isn't the source of undemocratic edicts, as a "controller of the narrative" his autocratic tweets encourage local politicians to do things like purge voter rolls, close polling places, and gerrymander voting districts to further their own exploitative interests.[13c]

Another writer tried to grasp his villainy; "He is Exhibit A of what happens when a country spends decades treating crimes by the poor as felonies and crimes by the powerful as misdemeanors,"[13d] which leads me down this same bombed-out road to a quote from Dostoyevsky: "The degree of civilization in a society can be judged by entering its prisons."[13e] Yet another story awaiting my immersion . . . and yours!

Meanwhile, I need a drink and some relief from my daily obsessing over your halfwit dipshit and the deteriorating state of your country.

June 22, 2018

This is beginning to feel like an online newsletter. I must say I take a perverse pleasure in being a technophobe — some would call me a Luddite because I don't do Facebook, Twitter, Instagram, or email; I don't even have a website. And forget about modems and routers and apps and iPads and algorithms and memes and bots. I prefer talking to you face to face. Some Earthling friends have urged me to start a blog, but I keep putting them off. Someday perhaps . . .

To continue: I was outraged when Pluto, for no good reason, reneged on his contract for Nancy Meehan and made her return to the Underworld. I nearly gave up the whole maddening project. What was the point of all these messianic gambits on my part, these fruitless intrusions into Earth's dead-end affairs, these nerve-wracking efforts on behalf of the luckless dead? But then I remembered something that has kept me going, at least for the short term. While I was down there negotiating for Nancy, I ran into John Cage, who hailed me with his famous axiom: "Why try to change the world? You'll only make things worse."[14] An assertion not to be taken lightly, mind you, but one with implications I have been slow to absorb. Even now, after all my flops, with diminishing resolve and about to conclude that I am not the right god for this mission, I am willing to take yet another stab at mitigating, if not changing, the worst tendencies and blunders you mortals can throw at me, quixotic as that may seem. So allow me to share with you some recent observations and efforts that may yet turn out to be of use to you.

1) For starters, let's talk about North Korea and a situation that seems to be shifting day by day. Before the fucking moron and the canny lunatic had their first summit meeting, I approached Kim Jong-un to ask him point-blank, "What do you want in the long run?" And taking off from there, I said: "I understand that it is all but impossible for you to back down and lose face when that asshole whoopee cushion of a president keeps upping the ante. But I can assure you that calling each other names in public like naughty schoolboys won't get you anywhere. I am sure that you are well aware that, according to most scientists, multi-city exchanges of nuclear detonations will bring on a new ice age. Spewing so much soot and dust into the stratosphere will cause a seventy percent reduction in sunlight reaching the Earth for decades. Crops will not grow; famine will ensue; Earth's populations will starve, including your own. For the sake of the world and your own populace, might you not cut the halfwit some slack by expressing your desires more openly? Like membership in what they call the "nuclear family"? Let's talk. Trade with South Korea without nuclear threat? Easy. Tickets to Radio City Music Hall and the pyramids and the Eiffel Tower? A snap. Doesn't

Pak Kil-yon, your U.N. ambassador, send you alluring descriptions of New York nightlife? Aren't you at all interested in *Hamilton* and how the rest of the world lives? There must be some space in your embattled psyche for a bit of curiosity and humility — unlike your appalling counterpart in the White House."

Following their first encounter I was surprised to learn that the whoopee cushion and the conniving despot had yet again gone into a bar together. This time around, the meeting achieved less than mutual flattery, and their cliffhanging chumminess produced nothing but a synchronized walkout. I know Kim couldn't just say to him, "Get off my back and I'll be a good boy," an unlikely request from someone whose concern over the size of his dick is beggared by that of the whoopee cushion.

After being confronted with the lunacy of these autocrats (who, as I write, have just had another meeting, this time to shake hands at the DMZ over nothing more substantial than shared publicity), I was dumbfounded to read the casually deployed language of certain sections of the U.S. male-dominated scientific community, which is supposedly serious about dealing with the threats of nuclear apocalypse. Their communications are larded with sexual metaphors, such as "vertical erector launchers," "thrust-to-weight ratios," "soft lay-downs," "deep penetration," "the comparative advantages of protracted versus spasm attacks," and what one military adviser to the National Security Council described as "releasing seventy to eighty percent of our megatonnage in one orgasmic whump."[15]

The psycho/social import of such reckless jargon is so grotesque that I can't allow myself even to begin to imagine the horrendous consequences. Meanwhile, holding the whole world hostage, the unhinged dipshit and wily dictator carry on their masquerade of wise leaders. Given that this relationship seems to change almost daily as the erratic imbecile's complicit handlers inside the White House attempt to keep up with — much less control — him, and feeling at my wit's end, I shall leave it at that while you all await the next installment.

2) Now I would like to mention some astonishing things that have been happening during my present visit. Women — and some men — of all classes and professions in the United States are coming out of the woodwork to reveal in unequivocal detail the egregious abuses previously pulled off by their male teachers, bosses, and co-workers.

Not that this kind of stuff is news to me. Olympus overruns with incidents in which the gods take advantage of their assistants and fellow gods and goddesses, as when Zeus forces Hera (a.k.a. Juno) or other deities — and sometimes even me! — to suck his cock while he's talking on his cell phone. Well, I could dismiss this particular kinkiness as "that's his thing," but of course he has others, like the ploy he sometimes uses to rape — let's call a spade a spade — yes, rape Danae and other young women in the form of, literally, a golden shower (whereas all I ever wanted — with him, at least — was a bit of frottage).

It behooves me at this point to confess to having been complicit in the not-so-distant past in some of Zeus's more outlandish erotic escapades, like the time, about a hundred years ago, when he and I were sitting in a car parked on the south side of West Eighth Street in New York City, he behind the wheel in a leather jacket and nose ring, in the guise of a beautiful 20-year-old young man, me beside him in female drag. So there we were, sitting in this car at midnight across the street from a brightly lit shop, and Zeus had opened the window on his side in order to make eye contact with a handsome older guy staring out from behind the shop-window. I asked Zeus, "Do you want me to leave or stay?" and he said, "Stay." So I stayed and — in deference to Zeus and one of my favorite authors, J. M. Coetzee, who wrote somewhere that "the prelude to the sexual act can be more desirable, more erotically fulfilling, than the act itself"[16] — I left Zeus to his thoughts and began scrolling through my newly acquired cell phone; and after awhile, sure enough, the guy comes out of the shop, crosses the street, goes around the car and gets in on my side, then slithers across my lap and, with half his body still on my lap, attaches himself to Zeus to deliver the anticipated blow job; and maybe because Zeus didn't seem to be enjoying the experience in that cramped space — the car was a 1965 Ford Mustang coupé — I kept whispering in his ear, "Say what you want, just say what you want."

I could run this story into the ground with more **lurid** details but won't risk boring you (ah-ha-ha!). All the same, allow me to add, for your amusement — or prurience, as the case may be — that just as he climaxed, Zeus ecstatically grabbed ***my* cell phone**! (OK, so this took place ***less*** than a hundred years ago; as I said before, it's hard to keep track of the passage of time these days.)

By now I've probably revealed more — or less! — than you ever wanted to know, while getting a bit sidetracked along the way.

Aside from the fact that the guy from the shop totally ignored my female presence — ran roughshow roughshod over me, as it were — the crux of the matter is that this was Zeus's setup, not mine, which is not to say that I'm passing judgment on him or it — nothing of the sort — I loved that Mustang! More to the point, I wish to emphasize, however circuitously, that the skewed and interlaced imbalances of power, privilege, entitlement, desire, intimidation, ambition, and consent — mutual and otherwise — can get played out in both weird and subtle ways. On the one hand, I have been amazed to hear that some Earthlings expose their penises to female colleagues in the workplace. It's hard to fathom what could possess anyone to do something like that! On the other, gestures which years ago would have been characterized as innocent touching now seem to have morphed into violations of personal space, and for good reason: Rather than being flattered or accommodating, women are stepping up to the plate to protest. Witness the recent accusations by several women about former U.S. vice president Joseph Biden's so-called affectionate but unsolicited physical overtures.[17]

Indeed, it is only recently that I myself have begun to face up to the creepiness and uncritical sense of entitlement manifested in the sadomasochistic sexual fantasies I've forced on my Muses (uh, but never while we're at work!). These antics should not be exempt from condemnation, and a mea culpa on my part may or may not be adequate in redressing such transgressions.[17a] But as I indicated earlier, I've been hoping for a modicum of atonement by way of all this earthly research and whatever insights and actions accrue from it. On the heels of the rapidly unfolding events down here, these efforts must now include bearing witness to how gods and men transpose their obsessive sex-in-the-head scenarios into obnoxious aggrandizement, which our two cultures both engender and shield from sight, emboldening you guys, when caught out, to ***trump***et in self-defense, "I thought she — or he — was willing," or "The situation has been 'mischaracterized,'" **OR**, even more damning, "I don't remember!" That Earthling women, however, keep coming forward in mind-boggling numbers to air explicit accounts of men's scummy and oblivious behavior — both past and present, at all levels of the social spectrum — that is what continues to bring me up short. As one woman I interviewed lamented, "The thing about the systematic reduction of a woman down to her parts is that she doesn't always know it's happening while it's going on. Just one day she wakes up and realizes that all she had was a face, a line of cleavage, two legs, a couple of hands, the swivel of her pelvis, the swell of her breast . . . like the disembodied parts in display windows."[17b] Which leads me to conclude that well before that awakening, being a girl anywhere on Earth must be a very bewildering experience. But it must also be bewildering for a boy. I am reminded of the words of a male writer on the "religion of masculinity":

> It is a compendium of saints: the vaunted patriarch, the taciturn cowboy, the errant knight, reluctant hero, gentle giant and omniscient father. . . . Fraternity, dominance, inflexibility, certitude — these are the commandments of male identity, the antediluvian constructs of masculinity that are easily weaponized in modern life.[17c]

I'm going to check in with Terpsichore to find out why she disappeared in such a rush following our last meeting. It's apparent, now that I'm thinking about it, that she was pissed off for more reasons than one and couldn't wait to escape from Earth — and me — fast enough. As soon as I get back, I will definitely encourage her to speak out on behalf of female Olympians and Earthlings everywhere, even if it lands me in the soup with Zeus. Let's hope some real and lasting changes will take place as a result, beyond all the current revelations that may yet, unfortunately, end up being a flash in the pan.

Apropos of the above, I am now remembering that the last time I was futzing around in the Underworld I ran into Ida Lupino, the remarkable Hollywood actress and director, and asked her to recommend a favorite movie that she herself had directed. She suggested *Outrage* from 1950. Believe it or not, it's about a rape and the repercussions for its victim. When I eventually caught a screening at the Museum of Modern Art in New York, I was surprised that this subject was being dealt with in Hollywood during such a retro era. It's not easy to watch. The writing and acting seem a bit stilted when compared to Hollywood's present-day penchant for rapid-fire, mealy jabbering, and the female protagonist continually runs into men who assault or manipulate her. Frankly, I had hoped she would marry the psychiatrist at the end and live happily ever after, but I have to admit the film was way ahead of its time, both for its subject matter and ambiguous, inconclusive ending. I strongly urge all you #MeToos to see it.

3) Then there's Myanmar, which is suddenly, maybe always has been, a hornet's nest. Aung San Suu Kyi, the foreign minister and state counselor — or whatever titles the generals use to avoid having to make her their president — after receiving a Nobel Peace Prize and endearing herself to the world, is now being reviled for her part in the barbarous expulsion of the Rohingya Muslims from her country, where they have lived for generations. It's possible I haven't been paying attention, but I was shocked to hear the term "ethnic cleansing" for the first time when told about this situation. Whether you characterize Suu Kyi's connection to the current brutality as detachment, passivity, collusion, helplessness, or political cunning, I can't help but agree with most people's negative judgment of her. I'd like to ask her, "Why is there not room in your country for other religions besides Buddhism? Talk to your generals; don't just stand by and let them pursue their murderous agenda. Whatever the limits of your power, use it for good."

I am aware that I may be simplifying the Myanmar situation and offering inept advice. But much as Suu Kyi can't be blamed for the misguided veneration heaped on her during her fifteen-year house arrest, I think if she continues to do nothing, she should be held accountable in the International Criminal Court in The Hague along with her generals, she for being more concerned with the well-being of her vicious, xenophobic dog than with that of the victims of ethnic cleansing, whose plight she ignores but must be all too aware of. I wonder how the Rohingya woman whose baby was snatched from her arms and thrown into the fire feels about Aung San Suu Kyi now.

[Sigh . . .] At this point I feel my outrage flagging. I'm just not up for another confrontation.

4) There is a catastrophe looming over your planet, which really should be number one in terms of urgency: global warming and its consequences. I need not belabor you with the entire roster of toxic causalities, like the fact that Robert E. Murray, the CEO of the largest coal company in the United States, and the fucking moron–appointed, disgraced administrator of the Environmental Protection Agency, Scott Pruitt, were in cahoots to roll back Obama's restrictions on the burning of fossil fuels while dismantling the very agency Pruitt's predecessors were charged to uphold. And under Pruitt's successor, former coal industry lobbyist and climate-change

denier Andrew Wheeler, the EPA will most likely continue to be a virtual subsidiary of the polluters it is supposed to regulate! As all rational people know, scientists' reports about the burning of fossil fuels and its link to global warming and the degradation of Earth's ecosystems are neither hoax nor conspiracy. What you probably *don't* know, which should alarm you, is that the concentration of carbon dioxide in the atmosphere is higher today than it has been in at least eight hundred thousand years, and more carbon has been released into the atmosphere since 1989, when one of the last international climate change conferences took place, than in the entire history of civilization preceding it.

Of course there are hordes of deniers, opportunists, and liars who contend that the current ecological situation on Earth is not any more dire than it was during previous periods of famine, war, drought, and plague, while many low-wage working people complain that their elitist opponents "are concerned with the end of the world while we are concerned with the end of the month."[18] To all of them I must protest that the stakes are higher now. The point of no return is at hand, a mere second as the history of the universe goes. And regardless of the opinion you may have of me, your Sun God, the deteriorating conditions in your oceans and atmosphere are neither my fault nor of my making; they are way beyond my control.

My digging in my heels finds an echo in another writer's lament:

> atmospheric and ocean warming, ocean acidification, sea-level rise, deglaciation, desertification, eutrophication — these are just some of the byproducts of our species' success. . . . There are only a handful of comparable examples in Earth's history, the most recent being the asteroid impact that ended the reign of the dinosaurs, sixty-six million years ago. . . . At this point, it might be prudent to scale back our commitments and reduce our impacts. But there are so many of us — nearly eight billion — and we are stepped in so far, return seems impracticable.

Elsewhere in the same essay she ironically cites the efforts of humankind to appeal to the gods and concludes with what I take to be a kind of backhanded exculpation of us: "It's hard to say who, these days, occupies Mount Olympus, if anyone."[18a]

All I can do to forestall your impending calamities is to try to persuade your scientists before it's too late to put all of their energies into exploring the joining of atoms through fusion as a substitute for the current practice of splitting atoms by fission. If successful, this will create a fuel source millions of times more powerful than the energy potential of oil and gas and substantially more effective than nuclear power. And then wouldn't you Earthlings be happy to say bye-bye to the carbon emissions of fossil fuels and the meltdown risks of your obsolete nuclear power plants![18b]

The significance and urgency of the above were brought home to me when I accompanied astrobiologist Nathalie Cabrol on an expedition into the forbidding high altitudes of Chile, where she was collecting samples of microbial organisms for research that might shed light on the history of life on Mars. At one point she stated:

> Earth itself is in no danger whatsoever. It will survive whatever humans throw at it. What *is* in danger is the environment that made human life possible. We are pretty much cutting off the branch we are sitting on. So either we understand that very quickly, or life will go on — but a different one.

Cabrol thinks the disappearance of life on Earth as you know it will not happen slowly. Her conclusion still rings in my ears: "It's going to be sudden and frightening."[18c, d]

Meanwhile, you folks in the United States are not only up to your eyeballs in those kettles of fish, but along with your ecological messes, you're in — to put it more profanely — even more deep shit, your political and economic disarray in high gear. One out of five children lives below the poverty line, a larger percentage than in any other industrialized nation. Half a million people are homeless on any given night. Over 80 million Americans have inadequate health insurance and one out of five cannot afford the prescription drugs they need. Even those of you white folks who see yourselves as progressive or enlightened have underestimated the relationship between economic and racial inequality and its consequences. The top one percent of U.S. families own forty percent of your country's wealth. Sixty-five percent of elected officials are white men, though they make up only thirty-one percent of the American population. And let me remind you that a larger sector of black Americans is currently imprisoned in the U.S. than black South Africans were during apartheid. And do you know that more than half of all black men without a high-school diploma go to prison at some time in their lives? Many white people I've met — and by some estimates a third of your country — are walled off in their ignorance or avoidance of such facts.

Insofar as there are no people of color on Olympus, and wanting to obtain more information about the source of U.S. Earthlings' blind spots around race, about eight decades ago I was privileged to accompany Zora Neale Hurston on a visit to 86-year-old Cudjo Lewis in his cabin near Mobile, Alabama; he was thought to be the last living African brought to America aboard a slave ship. Although Ms. Hurston knew him from a previous interview, we were sent away; he had no time for the past on that day. He wanted to work in his garden.[19]

On this current trip, I sought out an acquaintance whose story has subsequently kept me awake at night. She is an elderly white woman — for the sake of her privacy, let's call her Jane — who shared a memory from the late 1950s, when she was twenty years old and working in a New York office next to another typist, an older, somewhat overweight black woman. One day, about to discuss a bit of office business with her fellow worker, Jane addressed her with "How now, brown cow?"

At this point in the telling, Jane had an attack of amnesia, but she did recall that shortly thereafter she was filled with shame for having been oblivious to what might have been taken as a racial insult. She claimed that at the time she had meant no harm and had merely repeated a saying that she had remembered from a speech class she had attended to correct a long-standing speech impediment.[19a]

Back in the 1960s, my old friend the late psychoanalyst Joel Kovel might have described the above incident as an example of the "aversive" — or aversion-laden — racism of Northerners, in contrast to the dominating and violence-prone racism of 19th- and early-20th-century Southerners, the former characterized by ". . . coldness and the fantasy of dirt . . . the conflict between ideals and [bodily] disgust, a racism which in its many forms has become," as Kovel then saw it, "the central American dilemma of race relations."[19b]

I suspect that it was the beginning of the civil rights movement in the U.S. that spurred Jane's political awakening and a guilty self-consciousness that has shadowed her for well over half a century.

But despite my awareness of Kovel's theories and perhaps due to my growing friendship with Jane, I was willing to give her the benefit of the doubt and dismiss her misgivings as gratuitous self-laceration. In that she had no memory of her co-worker's response, her remark might have been received as offhand and careless rather than intentionally offensive. Nonetheless, regardless of how Jane has managed to process her long-ago gaffe, when the occasion arises, she now describes herself as a "permanently recovering racist."[19c] Which leads me to think that maybe I should do the same and not persist in not knowing what I know about my own racial acculturation.

A somewhat related feature of Jane's early history was brought home to me when she described her difficult childhood spent in foster homes, separated from her parents during World War II. She recounted looking out of a car window when she was about six years old:

> South of San Francisco we were passing the Tanforan racetrack where all the Japanese and Japanese-Americans were incarcerated. They had to sleep in the old horse stalls until being shipped off to permanent camps in Utah, Wyoming, and other states. I could see children my age staring out from behind the cyclone fence that surrounded their compound. The fences were capped with barbed wire. I was too young to understand the explanation that was offered, but at some level I knew these kids were like me: exiled and excluded.[19d]

I didn't press Jane on how the above memory might have affected her future relationships with African-Americans, but pursuing my own interests in such matters, I came across the comments of several writers regarding the history of slavery and racism in the U.S.: "Maybe not everyone who is white is a racist, but racism is what makes us white."[19e] From another point of view, "Slavery was not born of racism; rather, racism was the consequence of slavery."[19f] In response to the latter I thought the inverse may be equally valid, i.e., racism enabled and justified slavery. It is clear that whatever the viewpoint, they all bequeathed a pernicious legacy that has yet to be dismantled.

Stuart Hall has written: "We still have to explain why racial classificatory systems persist . . . we still have to account for why race is so tenacious in human history, so impossible to dislodge."[19g]

Not an answer to the above, but a poignant example of the magnitude of the problem jumped out at me when I read the following in an autobiography by an ex-slave:

> I spent the day gathering flowers and weaving them into festoons while the dead body of my father was lying within a mile of me. What cared my owners for that? He was merely a piece of property. Moreover, they thought he had spoiled his children, by teaching them to feel that they were human beings. This was blasphemous doctrine for a slave to teach, presumptuous in him, and dangerous to the masters.[19h]

Around this same time, I confessed my unease and preoccupations with this issue to a white acquaintance who — visibly exasperated — bellowed, "GET OVER IT! You're behaving like one of those obsessive people who seeks out endless sermons on anguish, guilt, and repentance!" Now I understand what she meant: Yes, don't ignore this stuff; get over it and do something. Jettison your self-pity and self-recriminations and stay alert. And maybe — in my case, at least — stay away from confusing theories! Now I'm thinking that the differences in attitude may be a generational thing. I have much to learn from these young ones, regardless of their skin color.

With such encounters and cautions percolating in my brain, I consulted Renée Green to ask for her thoughts from a black perspective. She wrote back, ". . . the conventional concept of race seems much too external and limited a description of what is in reality a multiple condition, even when an individual is perceived as black on a New York street . . ." She objected to being defined as a "single being," but, rather, referred to herself as a "combination person."[19i, j]

I subsequently had more conversations about race with both blacks and whites, some of them voicing silly racial stereotypes, like "black people eat lots of watermelon" and "white people put raisins in their potato salad." Inevitably, the chitchat took a more serious turn. A white woman revealed that she had experienced fear when passing a young black man in a hoodie on an empty street at night, and a black woman recounted an incident experienced by her son in his early adolescence: He was on his way home, carrying a package of fish she had asked him to buy for the family's dinner. It was raining, so he began to run. A police car cut him off at the corner and a white policeman jumped out with gun drawn and demanded that he raise his hands and drop the package. He complied; the package hit the ground and broke open, spilling its contents onto the sidewalk. Without a word, the cop got back in the car and drove off.[19k]

Reflecting on both of these stories — the "aversive" racist projection of the first one and the all-too-real confrontation in the second — I had no trouble deciding which narrator had more reason to be afraid. As poet Terrance Hayes has written, "You are beautiful because of your sadness. . . . You would be more beautiful without your fear."[19l]

Still seeking diverse points of view, I approached the comedian Tracy Morgan. In answer to specific questions he explained,

> I got funny to *survive*. Three things kept us [black people] from killing ourselves: jokes, music, and *fucking*. Why you think I became a comedian? I got funny 'cause it kept my mind away from being poor. Those hunger pains hurt, so I got funny. I'm *hungry* funny. That's what separated me from a lot of motherfuckers in my generation. That hunger.[19m]

His words, in their extremity and injury, stayed with me for days.

Later that same week Jane took me to see the revival of a film directed in 1980 by Bill Gunn called *Personal Problems*. Some of the situations in it seemed to be improvised, one of which kept me smiling whenever I thought of it in the following week. It was a scene of three young black women drinking in a New York outdoor cafe during the summer, and it struck me as a hilarious eye-opener into black female working-class camaraderie — all three talking at once, laughing, getting tipsy on glasses of wine, regaling and challenging one another with outrageous teasing and extravagant attitudinizing.

To someone like me just recently descended from the heights of Olympian provincialism, their boisterous interactions were an eye-opener, a rousing antidote to the white, culture-bound *meshegas* I have struggled to cast off. To put it more simply, I have been slow to grasp that people of color can be just as emotionally and intellectually complex as white people. Such an axiomatic declaration should be shouted from the rooftops, especially in view of your planet-wide racial conflicts. And beyond the issue of race, it would seem to me that navigating the other shifting goalposts of identity politics in the twenty-first century — be they gender, age, religion, sexuality, ethnicity, nationality — should not be used to pit your differences against each other. I'd like to see all of you working together as allies to achieve economic equality and reasonable contentment.

I'm not the only one who now and then harbors guarded hopes for solving your social quandaries. A long article about race in the New York Times concludes:

> If we could begin to grasp the limits of the planet we live on, if we could understand that the earth itself is an island and that we are all dependent on one another for survival, perhaps we would see each other differently . . . and have less use for the very idea of race.[20]

A big order, I admit, and since I seem to be in over my head here on Earth, for better or worse I'll have to leave such an enterprise to your professionals, especially after reading something by James Baldwin:

> . . . the rulers of the "higher races," struggling to hold on to what they have stolen from their captives . . . will precipitate a chaos throughout the world which, if it does not bring life on this planet to an end, will bring about a racial war such as the world has never seen.[21]

[Sigh . . .] Sorry, now that I've become so invested in Earthlings' affairs, I can't seem to strike a balance in this rambling screed between hope and despair. Fed up to here with Olympian hypocrisies and shenanigans, I was expecting something different down here, disingenuous as that may seem.

After writing the above, I recalled something indeed different, at least for me. While coming downtown on the A train in New York City, I was reading another article in the New York Times. (By now you've probably surmised — correctly! — that the NYT is my favorite reputable source of news.) In fact, I had just read the line "Noticing difference is not the same thing as hating difference"[21a] when, looking up, I saw opposite me a white man sitting next to a small child who couldn't have been much older than three. The boy was wearing glasses and his facial coloring was almost jet black. I assumed the man was the child's adoptive father because he was so attentive and affectionate with him. Filled with admiration, I thought, "What a huge responsibility, having to protect your black child while guiding him through the racial thickets of America." Immediately my critical faculties kicked in with, "Would it be any different if the father was black?"

Oy, I'll give myself a break and leave this question for you New Yorkers to answer.[21b, c, d]

Shortly thereafter, another incident unsettled me. I was on my way into Manhattan from JFK in a cab. The cabbie was caught up in a traffic jam at a red light on an offshoot of the freeway and had carelessly come too close to a car full of young black men. One of them came around to my driver's side, motioned him to roll down his window, and asked, "You have a problem?" at the same time making a threatening hand gesture at waist level in and out of his unzipped jacket. The meaning was clear: He had a gun. The cabbie mumbled something and stared impassively ahead. Fortunately, the situation didn't escalate. The guy got back into his car and drove off as the light changed. Whether or not my black driver had "a problem," by this time I had no doubts that your country has one, in spades, so to speak. (Please forgive my careless colloquialism, which, in this day and age, may read as racist!)

On a much different note I asked Jane about some dancers she had worked with in the early 1970s.[22] She obliged with enthusiasm: "We were a rollicking, mismatched, anarchic, competitive bunch that had been exposed to the social upheavals of the 1960s. All highly trained dancers, when we went on tour we thought of ourselves as a kind of rock-and-roll dance collective. There was no dominating choreographer, and we had no patience with rehearsing one another's movement ideas, so we gave all that up, and when we hit the performance arena we were transformed into improvisational geniuses. There's been nothing like it since."

I urged her to go on: "Could you be more specific?"

"Oh, I don't remember that much," she said, "I only lasted two years — the pressure of making stuff up on the spot was too much for me; I couldn't do it without getting stoned — but the rest of them went on for another four or five years. From what I've heard and seen, the audiences either adored them or walked out, too mired in their outdated conceptions of 'dance' to risk absorbing something new. The great thing about the group was that anyone could initiate anything, galvanizing the others to jump in and spontaneously expand on a particular *shtick*. Both spectators and performers never knew what would happen next: sofas, music, pillows, talk, puns, insults, costumes, props, wordplay, and movement galore, you name it; nothing was out of bounds and everyone was up for the unpredictable disruptions. I recently saw a film of their last performance and was green with envy not to have been there!"

After that, for some reason, Jane shut up like a clam and refused to answer more questions, so I guess I'll have to satisfy my curiosity elsewhere — that is, if I'm down here long enough. I didn't get a chance to ask her about her involvement with an earlier group of performers that has recently been accused of racism,[23] a familiar can of worms that I know she will have to deal with. I now feel in a better position to help her out.

But getting back to my astonishment at your seemingly intractable American or, more accurately, United States muddles — racial inequality being only one among many — the Koch brothers, those finagling chemical- and oil-industry overlords, through their hand-in-glove sway over your sinister vice president, are well on their way to sticking over a hundred of their own unqualified and malleable people into instrumental government positions in the EPA and Department of the Interior, and the witless whoopee cushion will never notice or, worse, doesn't care. He's probably too busy trying to pander to that Russian plutocrat Putin and too busy being fêted and sucked up to by the Saudis and too busy authorizing a $110 billion sale of arms to the latter, including the precision-guided missiles with which they have destroyed hospitals and killed hundreds of innocent men, women, and children in Yemen. He's also busied himself with making it easier for employers to refuse to include birth control in their health-care plans while reinstating the "global gag rule" on abortion counseling and undermining the World Health Organization's advocacy in underdeveloped countries for breast milk by supporting the bullying baby-formula industries that so predictably fancy profits over women's health. And what about his fuck-you to two hundred thousand Salvadorans and almost sixty thousand Haitians by rescinding deportation protections previously granted to them, and his efforts to roll back protections for gay and transgender people? And now he's busy blaming U.S. gun carnage on crazy people instead of the National Rifle Association and the craven politicians it supports, including the unhinged asshole himself, who, if he's allowed his druthers, would supply all your public-school teachers with guns. (I'll bet you don't realize that in the United States guns have been responsible for the deaths of more civilians than all the wars in which your country has been involved since its inception.) Come to think of it, how about arming not only all those teachers but every man, woman, and adolescent in the U.S. with AR-15 assault rifles?!

Yes, the shameless schmuck's calendar is full. Between such maneuvering and unpredictable, infantile, early-morning tweets and his temper tantrums and starting an international trade war, while whining, "It's just so unfair that American companies aren't allowed to pay bribes to get business overseas,"[24] he has hardly any time left for creating havoc among international allies and maligning the free press and firing his cabinet members and replacing them with even more extremist reprobates and getting the U.S. into an ever deeper immigration imbroglio and praising despots and being flattered by servile creeps and applauded by the "trumpenproletariat."[24a]

I shouldn't come down too hard on the latter; I've been thinking that their vote for the asshole, even as it was against their own interests, was propelled less by conviction than by disillusion with his predecessors and disgust with the status quo. The evidence clearly shows that, rather than a previously homogeneous group, they constitute a bloc of affluent older white people and poorer white voters. As a British writer argued in a provocatively titled essay:

> . . . the invisible glue that holds these pacts together is physical pain. A third or more of adults in the US and UK report that they are "often" in pain. Most elderly people experience regular pain anyway, but so do the poor, since inequality makes people a lot sicker than they might otherwise be.[24b]

In contrast, there was the New York taxi driver who answered my question "Why did you vote for him?" with "He makes me laugh." It's hard to believe that to many of the scoundrel's followers, the U.S. government is a laughing matter. Somehow, I find the Brit's explanation more to the point: A disparate group, though economically dissimilar, is unified in physical pain.

(Second thoughts: To what degree were any of them aware of this? And if they were, did they think Rump would make the pain go away? Oh dear . . . The title of the above essay says it all: "Can the Poor Think?")

I stumbled over more evidence of your prime prevaricator's popular appeal in another author's remarks:

> Out of all the American Presidents, he is the only one whose speeches I can understand directly, without translation; there are no big words or complicated grammar. Everything he says is reduced to the simplest possible formulation.[24c]

Recently, after reading the depositions of Michael Cohen, your would-be mobster's former hatchet man, I wondered how an otherwise intelligent person could have allowed himself to serve a borderline illiterate who describes himself as "an extremely stable genius" yet would fail a sixth-grade reading comprehension test. I was at a loss to account for how Cohen had carried out his boss's criminal directives for a whole decade without having second thoughts. His explanation that his proximity to power was "intoxicating" is telling. Be that as it may, I, for one, hope your bureaucrats and prosecutors can pin more than one thing on the scurrilous sexist racist swindler and make it stick after Special Counsel Robert Mueller's final un-redacted report is revealed the House Democrats' impeachment efforts pay off, and and before your slow creep toward fascism reaches a heartrending end point.

The German philosopher Peter Sloterdijk has called Rump a "degenerate sheriff" and adds, "He channels global feelings of ecological doom . . . but instead of waiting for a crisis to impose a ruling, his rulings get him the emergencies he needs. The playground for madness is vast," which leaves all of you — and, surprisingly, even me — susceptible to his "rage entrepreneurship."[25] Actually, I doubt if the word "ecological" can be found in the degenerate sheriff's vocabulary. With his xenophobic predisposition — and under the fraudulent rationale of national security — he sees threats not from ecological catastrophe but from ***EYERYONE***, with the exception of sycophants, dictators, and his white constituency — the latter benighted, bamboozled, and, hopefully, soon to have regrets.

Comparing the current U.S. situation to that in Germany before the Nazis took power, another writer I recently encountered has offered an eerie analogy:

> Thinking about the end of Weimar democracy as the result of a large protest movement colliding with complex patterns of elite self-interest, in a culture increasingly prone to aggressive mythmaking and irrationality — strips

> away the exotic and foreign look of swastika banners and goose-stepping Storm Troopers. Suddenly, the whole thing looks [all too] close and familiar.[26]

(Incidentally, it is a known fact and not coincidental that before becoming president, your malevolent leader had a copy of *Mein Kampf* on his nightstand, undoubtedly more for inspiration than research!)

Compounding the above, my friend Monica, in a characteristic hissy fit, wrote the following to me:

> Rump has pretty much made everything — other than registering Democrats — seem inconsequential. So no wonder art holds less appeal. I think this period will go down as one of the least productive periods of our collective lives . . . as we renew our news feed every five minutes, respond psychically to relentless Republican/Rump terrorism, fear the calamity of our erupting democracy, realize we have no suitable coping mechanisms for the repressive aggression of white men (and women), awaken to the undeniable reality of climate change (during a period of inexplicable coal renewal in the US and immoral EPA rollbacks), witness treason live on TV. . . . The incomprehensible unfurls moment by moment before our eyes. How can one envision anything abstract, like art, in this hellscape?[27]

I dare you folks to cram all that and much, much more into your pipes and smoke it! You have a hardworking president, and he's got you by the short hairs, even as he himself is in almost as many crosshairs. His cronies are going down, and the self-styled mob boss is next. Meanwhile, he's in your hands, Millennials, and I'm counting on youse to overcome. I just wish you very old ones — you who are stalked by the memory of an age of revolution in the 1960s — if only you old ones might hang on long enough to see the world without him and his vile legacy.[28]

For the time being, please be a little indulgent with my soupçon of sarcasm. After keeping glued to your news feeds with their daily plot twists, I'm in the grip of one of my chronic-fatigue days. Like many of you, I can't afford to miss one episode or I'll be left behind. If I, an Olympian God, can feel so besieged, I can well imagine the stress that you Earthlings must be experiencing. I got a glimpse of this when an acquaintance down here recounted a dream she had in which I was a protagonist:

> You and I were at some kind of karaoke bar, hiding. But then you decided to sing, although you rejected everything on their playlist. You came up with your own song, some kind of show tune, very Rodgers-and-Hart-ish, but the lyrics were all about Kierkegaard. You were creating impressively on-point arguments in rhyme. I wish I could remember what they were; the only thing that's lasted with me was that you paired "existence" with "resistance" and "Camus" with "fuck you." The crowd went bonkers for it.[29]

After watching TV news late one night and feeling assaulted by an especially outrageous update on your creepy asshole's offenses, I too had a dream: A group of people enter a performance space and stand in a row, shoulder to shoulder, facing the audience. I instruct each of them to hurl a brief invective at the fucking narcissist seated in the front row and then exit, one at a time. But the row grows longer and longer as more and more people show up, and those newly arrived haven't heard my instructions, so I must keep repeating them. The situation is out of control and seems interminable until I manage, mercifully, to wake up and put a stop to it.

And last night I had an even more disturbing and mysterious dream: I am attending a dinner party in the embodiment, yet again, of Yvonne Rainer. I am seated at a large, round table in a fancy restaurant somewhere in Switzerland. On my right is Peter Wollen and to my left is a wealthy patron of the arts. She and I are wearing identical pink skirt suits and pillbox hats à la Jackie Kennedy on the day JFK was assassinated. Mine, not hers, is splattered with blood. The arts patron is trying to make small talk with me, but I am sunk in a deep depression, unable to respond or move. Peter Wollen leaves in frustration, and soon the woman gives up and also leaves the table. When Wollen returns, he tries to console me by observing that "Switzerland has even more filthy-rich people per capita than the United States."

Has it really come to this: that enactments of Earthlings' distress are showing up in the dreams of Olympians? It's been proven beyond a doubt that you dream of *us*, but why must *my* dreams be swamped by your problems? Isn't it enough that I have volunteered to deal with you during my waking hours? Pardon my irritation, but today I am overwhelmed with sadness and a sense of futility. I keep thinking about Polyhymnia's exhortation to leave the befouled planet before it's too late, which reminds me of a line from that play by . . . what's-his-name? — (Oh, gimme a break; even gods have memory lapses!) — um . . . Tony Kushner! He's the one who wrote, "Before life on Earth becomes finally merely impossible, it will for a long time have become completely unbearable."[30]

Divertissements:
It's time for a breather from portents of the coming apocalypse by way of an interesting tidbit in the Times about the discovery of singing mice found high in the mountains of Central America. The voicings of these tiny rodents actually have "profound similarities to our own conversations!"[31] Reading that article was like immersing myself in a warm bath.

Another respite occurred when I visited a New York gallery that was showing a multiscreen video installation by the British artist Isaac Julien that dealt with Frederick Douglass, the American ex-slave and abolitionist.[32] I was again surprised at being moved to tears when on one screen Douglass walks serenely in slow motion beside a black horse while on another, two white women in mid-19th-century outfits crouch on the seashore and inscribe in the sand: "Send back the money," a reference to compensation owed and still not paid to ex-slaves and their descendants one hundred and fifty-five years after Emancipation. The power of the installation was not diminished, but only enhanced, by the contrast between its visual beauty and virulent history.

For more relief from my obsessions with the unraveling daily news, I turned myself into a fly on the wall in the home of Mildred and Doris, two quirky old friends I've known for almost forty years, and caught an episode of what I'll call "The Mildred and Doris Show."

> M and D are reading different sections of the New York Times in their living room from their respective vantage points on sofa and lounge chair. M starts to get up and D offers her the TV remote.
>
> M: No thanks, I have to put my dinner together.
> D: Oh, I thought you were getting up to turn on the evening news.

M: Well, you were mistaken. But I'm going to need your seat when I'm through cooking.
D: I know; when I see you coming out of the kitchen with your tray, I'll gird my loins and move from sofa to chair.
M: I don't think you mean that.
D: What? "Girding my loins" or giving up the sofa?
M: (*Gesturing to her thighs*) "Girding the loins" refers to protecting this part of the body with armor.
D: Oh, not the crotch? Maybe I used the wrong expression. But I can't think of a better one; to me, "girding one's loins" suggests alertness, readiness . . .
M: No, it means preparing for battle.
D: Ha! Then it's not that far from the truth!

On this occasion Doris had the last word.

Yet another reprieve from catastrophic news came on the heels of an edifying TV show about a cure for sickle-cell anemia through the introduction of the HIV virus into the human bloodstream, a procedure that actually spooks deviant red blood cells into behaving themselves. And to similar salutary effect, Jane Goodall put some of your earthly dilemmas into perspective for me when last I saw her, in fact as recently as two weeks ago in her favorite Manhattan diner after I had arrived late and breathless from taking an ill-advised shortcut and climbed one hundred and thirty steps in Hudson Heights to get there.

For the moment, allow me a brief aside: Before climbing those steps, I had emerged from the depths of the A train into blinding sunlight — Calliope and Melpomene, despite their discontents, were apparently still fulfilling their obligations — and asked two people waiting at the crosswalk for directions. As I thanked them and was turning away, I heard, "Could you spare something for food?" Turning back and examining them more closely, I saw that they were a youngish white man and woman, shabbily dressed and, I suspected, homeless; so I fished out the smallest bill in my wallet — ten dollars — and put it into the hands of the woman, who looked at it incredulously. I wished them good luck and went on my way, wondering how two young white people could have gotten into such a pickle and regretting that I hadn't had the time to inquire further.

On reaching Jane's diner, we had a good chat over BLTs. Charming and sweet-natured as ever, she said, just before parting,

"What can we do to help this gloomy situation? I meet so many incredible people doing amazing things, saving animals on the brink of extinction, restoring the forest, cleaning up a river. It's knowing what can be done that gives people the courage to fight."[33]

Yes, "knowing what can be done" is key. I think this is as good a time as any for me to bow out of Earthlings' travails and leave you to manage things on your own. After all my griping and nitpicking, I still have confidence in your resilience, ingenuity, and compassion. I wish all of you the utmost fortitude to hold off the decline — and in the worst-case scenario, the end — of your world and the lives of those dear to you. With that said, and to the extent that I myself will never mean much more to you than a figment of your fears, fantasies, and wishful thinking, I'm almost out of here.

Not . . . so . . . fast! Forgive me for detaining you just a mite longer with a few afterthoughts: In the early 1950s I spent a number of months on Earth in the guise of a 17-year-old attending his first and only year of college. While there I took a course in Western philosophy and became deeply involved in the writings of Plato, Bishop Berkeley, Bertrand Russell, and Hannah Arendt, among others. However, in contrast to the gutsy indigenous Canadian who wrote, "I wanted as much of the world as I could take, and I didn't have the conscience to be ashamed."[34] I must confess with no little embarrassment that following that first year, although I did well, I dropped out. As that depressed teenager and for reasons then unknown to me, I could barely admit to wanting anything, and I *did* have a sense of shame, only in my case, I was ashamed of abandoning my formal education, a decision that, on occasion, I have continued to regret. Under other circumstances I might have aspired to become a literary giant or philosopher or statesman here on Earth, but the cards were stacked, and when a vacancy came up, I applied for and settled into the more modest occupation of Solar Charioteer. This most recent visit, however, has once more brought me face to face with my fate, and here again I find myself crashing against the shoals of my aborted earthly ambitions. As I've said before, the past is never dead. If it doesn't grab you by the throat, it gives you a royal kick in the ass.

I fear that this angst-ridden rant will raise questions — if not hackles — that I will be ill-equipped to address, and by presenting myself as an artist — which I frequently do when I'm down here — I risk being unmasked and accused of fraud or, at the very least, of opportunism. I can't help wondering how many real artists get away with murder. In the popular imagination they play it like it lays and then slink away from the storms brought on by their marks. ("Who, me? How do you expect *me* to figure out how to change the world or solve its problems?")

Whether or not I am able to pull off my artist impersonation, be it male or female, whenever I'm down here I inevitably find myself ricocheting from catastrophe to absurdity, from chaos to elation, from desperation to Keystone Kops, while being pummeled by the sheer volume of human actions "in a world torn asunder by the arbitrary and anxiously defended borders of statehood and masculinity."[35, 35a]

Under such chaotic conditions, what on this Earth can I do for you people? What more can I say? Except to confess that I am inordinately attracted to people who can't finish their sentences, as if they are perpetually trying to get ahead of the game to avoid criticism or punishment. A tic from childhood, I'm sure.

After careful consideration, and much as I hate to abandon youse guys, I've decided to heed Polyhymnia's advice at long last. Unlike Sisyphus, *I've* not been condemned to hang out down here and nurse my frustrations for all of eternity. Having spilled my guts in this protracted tirade, I should cut my losses and go home before I succumb to the disorder that a Portuguese writer described in a poem:

> What kind of magic potion
> Did you give me from that jar?
> That I forget who I am
> But always know who you are . . .[36, 37]

In need of a final bit of advice, I dropped in to the Underworld for another chat with Walter Benjamin. He supplied me with what seemed at the time like a cryptic coda, but which I now see as highly pertinent to my unresolved experiences here on Earth:

> The path you wanted to take
> The letter that you wanted to write
> The man that you wanted to rescue
> The seat that you wanted to occupy
> The woman that you wanted to follow
> The word that you wanted to hear

> The door that you wanted to open
> The costume that you wanted to wear
> The question that you wanted to pose
> The hotel room that you wanted to have
> The opportunity that you wanted to seize[38]

Benjamin's laconic plea inspired me to collage some of my favorite lines from the same source:

> dream and tree
> to gain clarity
> in the horror
> One step ahead of me lay the sea
> like a field which had been painfully plowed,
> already sown with the seeds of my later life
> while the beam of the moon would alienate
> its most familiar details from me —
> Coming closer and closer, it tore the earth apart.
> Then I recovered and went home.[38a]

Now that I'm contemplating going home, it has occurred to me that a happy outcome of my latest extended sojourn on your planet is that I can finally allow myself a wee bit of pride in my function in the universe. But not before I quote one more treasure from my beloved and tragic Walter — a poignant example of one of his lifelong concerns:

> A Klee drawing named "Angelus Novus" shows an angel looking as though he is about to move away from something he is fixedly contemplating. His eyes are staring, his mouth is open, his wings are spread. This is how one pictures the Angel of History. His face is turned toward the past. Where we perceive a chain of events, he sees one single catastrophe that keeps piling ruin upon ruin and hurls it in front of his feet. The angel would like to stay, awaken the dead, and make whole what has been smashed. But a storm is blowing from Paradise; it has got caught in his wings with such violence that the angel can no longer close them. The storm irresistibly propels him into the future to which his back is turned, while the pile of debris before him grows skyward. This storm is what we call progress.[38b]

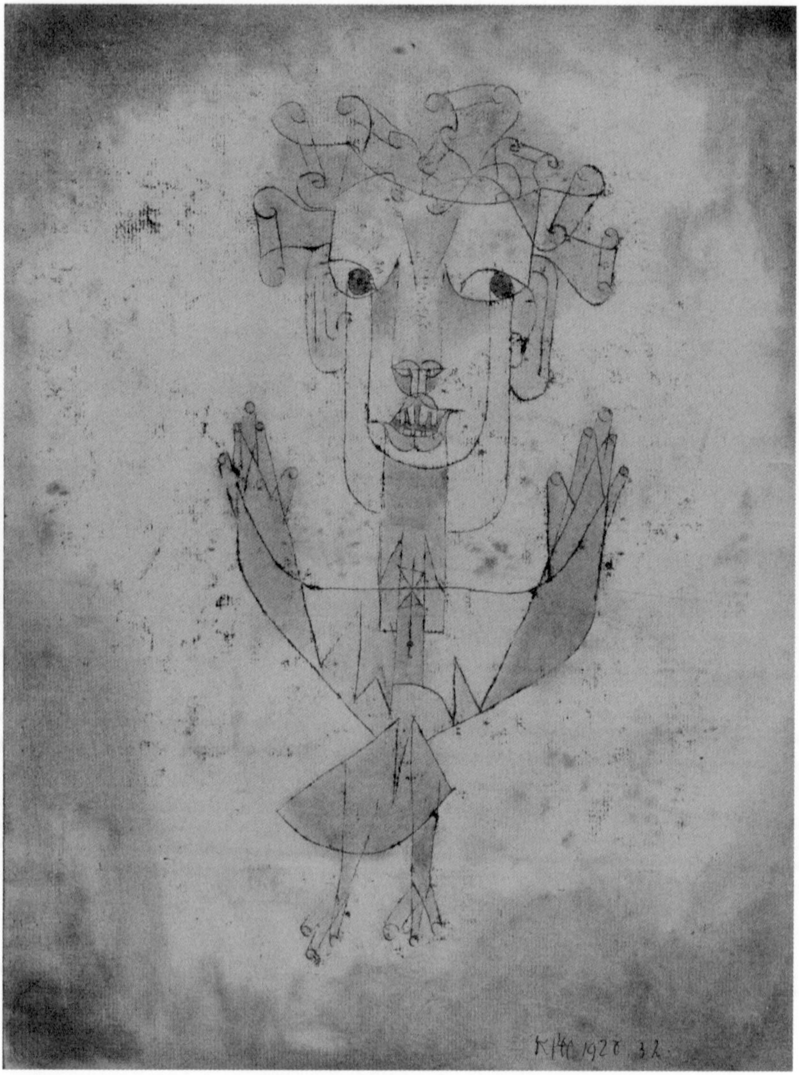

Paul Klee, *Angelus Novus*, 1920.
Collection of the Israel Museum, Jerusalem.
Photo by Elie Posner, courtesy the Israel Museum, Jerusalem.

Which brings me to a question that has been lurking all this while in the back of my mind: What would you guys do without my daily excursions across the heavens? There will be many days when my travels up there will comfort you, even while yours down here, unfortunately, will rarely comfort me.[39]

All right, I am almost done. Though it may have seemed like a long goodbye, this time I mean it. Not wanting to leave on the wrong foot, however, I shall propose a temporary respite from your quandaries and steer you to a favorite Laurel and Hardy short, which I consider quite germane to these troubled times. It's called *Big Business*, directed in 1929 by Leo McCarey, and you can find it on YouTube. I am confident it will elicit restorative laughter and buoy your spirits.

And by the way, please ignore Gustave Flaubert's *bon mot*, "Just when the gods had ceased to be, and the Christ had not yet come, there was a unique moment in history, between Cicero and Marcus Aurelius, when man stood alone."[40] I beg to differ: You humans have never been alone. And as far as the gods are concerned, I'm still around — in one form or another[41] — if only to remind you of your brutal histories, random swerves, and ultimate demise, no less than the dangers of your nostalgia, resentments, anger, and fear.

Finally, allow me one last quote, this time from a former "red diaper baby," writing in 1974, when he was about thirty years old:

> We're not a lost, damned, corrupt generation. We're the future, we've got hope, discipline, dedication. We're not cynics or victims. We don't expect Utopia but we're not disenchanted. We don't anticipate the Millennium or the Apocalypse, but we're not pessimists.[42]

Oy gevald! I wonder if he's still around, and, if so, what he would think of the Rump era and the gloomy prospect that humans will have finally killed and consumed every last living thing on Earth. Even while heaving a doleful sigh, however, I can't help but applaud all you survivors of trauma and cultural wars, hoarding your victories and counting your sores.

Most sincerely,
Apollo Musagète
February 3, 2020

P.S.: Just before leaving Earth, I took a long walk up to Fort Tryon Park in New York City to look out over the mighty Hudson. You folks are so fortunate; we don't have anything like that on Mount Olympus![43, 44, 45]

P.P.S.: And earlier, on that dark and dreary shore of the New York subway system, a total stranger and I hurtled in tandem down the stairs and into the train with not a second to spare. As the doors closed behind us, we shared a triumphant exchange of giddy grins and high fives across our gendered and racial divides. Only after I had found a seat did "the dead and gone come swarming up around me, each asking about the grief that touched them most."[46]

Yet another New York story.

DESULTORY AFTERTHOUGHTS

January 11, 2020

Today I was moved almost to tears by a piece in the Metropolitan section of the NY Times, page 2 "Sunday Routine" about a guy named Jule Hall who, having spent 22 years in prison, now 44, works for the Ford Foundation as a consultant. Most of these accounts are of white people who use their Sundays for socializing with family and friends. Hall, seemingly content and grateful, describes solitary activities like bike-riding, laundry, and Starbucks coffee-drinking, prison memories always close at hand—a black man, no doubt.

Reading *East West Street* by Philippe Sands, whose grandfather, Hersh Lauterpacht, born in Poland in 1897, ended up a law professor in the U.S. Sands's mother was spirited out of Europe as a baby by an anti-Nazi named Elsie Tilney. Lauterpacht was responsible for the concept of "crimes against humanity" leveled at the Nazis after WWII. The other main protagonist in this book is Rafael Lemkin, the author of the "genocide" concept, also used in the prosecution of Nazis. The reach of Sands's writing is far-ranging as he travels all over Europe for archival research and interviews.

February 13, 2020

Well, folks, having been given reluctant permission by Zeus, it looks like I'm back for a while—I can't seem to keep my hands off you people, especially in the U.S. Roaming around New York, my eye catches relatively insignificant things, like the woman with two dogs, one of which is bundled up to the ears against the cold while the other is hairless and bereft of coat. And of course, far more consequential, is the despicable behavior of Rump now that he has escaped impeachment. As if, as Senator Susan Collins from Maine avowed, "He's learned his lesson." Quite the contrary: He now feels impervious and has even said, "I can do anything I want!" Again? What's next?

I don't understand why writers on this planet use terms like "humanity" and "dehumanizing" to exalt or deplore your inescapable existential condition, as though you have a choice of existence down here other than "human." Another irritating ploy is "universal"—Gimme a break: you guys don't know the half of what's out there and where I come from!

February 14, 2020

Riffling through Yvonne Rainer's papers, I found this curious piece, probably referring to something she did in a London gallery around 2014:[47]

Who's up; who's down; who's in the middle? The worker/designer from the London gallery flew all the way to Scotland to show her—and I'm talking about me, the more up one—to show her what he was going to do. Then he did it, and on time to boot. But he wasn't invited to the dinner following the opening. You heard me: He wasn't invited to the dinner. In fact he wasn't even *at* the opening. His work was done. Par for the course in the art world.

Much later she flew back to London and was introduced to the male technician, or straw boss, who probably held the place together, then to the three male workers, then to the real boss, then to the four office workers, all women. There seems to be a progression, or odd distribution, here of cheerfulness and affability that correlates with one's gender, function, and contingent social status: At the top, on a scale of 1 to 10 with 10 being the most affable, the owner/financier a 10 in cheeriness, the straw boss a 7 or 8, the glum male workers a 3, whereas the upstairs office team predictably matches the owner in cheeriness, naturally or unnaturally, most likely due to their gender. As women, they're bound to be cheerful no matter what.

And she? What's her stake in the cheeriness sweepstakes? I must say the affability of the sponsor/owner/financier drew her out of her accustomed torpor/grumpiness. After all, she was the star, the celeb, the privileged one, a status made even more enhanced by her longevity. She was the legend, the ancient one, the survivor, most of her marbles intact, if not her optimism. She couldn't say she had seen it all, only just enough to complain that all that she had ever wanted to change had come to nothing more than standing still, or something like that. But I won't bore you further with this cantankerous character. As someone famously said: Let's move on.

March 9, 2020

Reading a review of Thomas Piketty's new book, "Capital and Ideology," I am struck by the critic's summary: "He tries to expose the contradictions of 'hypercapitalism' with a breathtaking series of reforms, including a schedule of taxation on income and wealth that reaches ninety per cent and the elimination of nation-states in favor of 'a vast trans-national democracy,' which will secure a universal right to education and a capital endowment, free circulation of people, and de facto virtual abolition of borders."[48] Well, my friends, in frustration and resignation, I'll leave you to it!

Inspired by Emily Coates's *Incarnations*, performed at Danspace, New York, March 16, 17, 18, 2017. With thanks to physicist Sarah Demers and Gregg Bordowitz, and with boundless gratitude to Martha Gever for her editorial advice and patience and to Su Friedrich, Ruth Rainero, Wendy Perron, and others who re;ad early versions and excerpts during Apollo's extended forays on Earth.

Please note: Yvonne Rainer (not Apollo) is responsible for the following notes and observations.

1. Adapted from Adam Gopnik's essay on Romain Gary's fabulism, "The Made-Up Man," *New Yorker*, January 1, 2018, p. 68.

2. Yuval Noah Harari, "Why Fiction Trumps Truth," *New York Times*, May 26, 2019.

2a. Édouard Louis, *The End of Eddy* (New York: Farrar, Straus, and Giroux, 2017). Reviewed by Garth Greenwell, *New Yorker*, May 8, 2017, p. 62.

3. It was the British writer Will Self who, in the *New Statesman* in 2016, used the epithet "enigma wrapped inside a whoopee cushion" to deride Boris Johnson, then the U.K. foreign secretary; and Rex Tillerson, former U.S. secretary of state, who was heard muttering "fucking moron" as he emerged from a meeting with the fucking moron. Apollo uses both terms — and others, of course — as opprobrium throughout this essay to identify only one person, with no intent to offend anyone else, at least not with those two forms of abuse.

4. A week after Hurricane Maria laid waste to Puerto Rico in 2017, in an expression of utter contempt, he threw rolls of paper towels into the San Juan crowd, as if to say, "Let them eat paper towels while they're mopping up," and later rebuked them for not taking care of themselves. This deplorable spectacle, followed by his references to Haiti, El Salvador, and some African nations as "shithole countries," dispelled any lingering doubt in Apollo's mind that our fucking moron whoopee cushion of a president is an autocratic racist. Shortly thereafter,

Apollo came down with another attack of chronic-fatigue syndrome.

5. Kwame Anthony Appiah, "Stonewall and the Myth of Self-Deliverance," *New York Times*, June 23, 2019.

5a. Umberto Eco, "Ur-Fascism," *New York Review of Books*, June 22, 1995, p. 9.

6. Amiri Baraka (LeRoi Jones), "In Memory of Radio," in *Preface to a Twenty-Volume Suicide Note* (New York: Totem Press/Corinth Books, 1961).

7. Nicolas Jacques Pelletier, a highwayman, was guillotined outside the Hôtel de Ville in the Place de Grève. The last execution by guillotine took place as recently as 1977!

7a. Anna Furse, "An Anatomy Act," in *I Am Not a Piece of Meat*, compilation archive–interactive site, "Create Ireland": http://www.iamnotapieceofmeat.com/.

7b. Bret Stephens, *New York Times*, August 11, 2018.

7c. *60 Minutes*, CBS-TV, August 19, 2018.

7d. Thomas Gibbons-Neff, "Mission Inscrutable: My Tours in Afghanistan," *New York Times*, September 17, 2019.

8. Renée Green, *William Morris*, 2011, letterpress and digital print paraphrasing an excerpt from William Morris's *A Dream of John Ball*, shown in Green's exhibition *Pacing: Within Living Memory* at the Carpenter Center for the Visual Arts at Harvard University, Cambridge, Massachusetts, 2018.

8a. Adam Gopnik, "Diderot Dicta," *New Yorker*, March 4, 2019, p. 54.

9. Trisha Brown, American dancer and choreographer, 1936–2017.

10. Nancy Meehan, American dancer and choreographer, 1931–2017.

11. Ian White, British performance artist, writer, curator, 1971–2013.

12. Please forgive the inconsistencies and apparent contradictions in Apollo's narrative, especially regarding the topics of death and the afterlife, human mortality and the Underworld. I have yet to question him on these and related subjects.

13. Summit meeting in Helsinki on July 16, 2018, at which Trump accepted Putin's denial of Russian interference in the 2016 U.S. election.

13a. Nicholas Kristof: "We Will Survive, Probably," *New York Times*, March 7, 2019.

13b. Frank Bruni, "Will the Media Be Trump's Accomplice Again?", *New York Times*, January 13, 2019.

And more to the point: "But Trump chaos, both intentional and otherwise, has proved a great de facto political strategy, precisely because we are *neurologically incapable of handling it.*" Jennifer Senior, "Our Brains Can't Handle the Trump Era," *New York Times*, February 10, 2019; italics hers.

13c. Casey Cep, "Finish the Fight! The Halting, Imperfect, Unfinished Work of Women's Suffrage," *New Yorker*, July 8 and 15, 2019, p. 64.

13d. Alex Kingbury, "Editorial Observer," *New York Times*, March 2, 2019.

13e. Dwight Garner: "Locked Down No More," review of *Solitary: Unbroken by Four Decades in Solitary Confinement, My Story of Transformation and Hope*, by Albert Woodfox with Leslie George, *New York Times*, March 5, 2019.

14. John Cage, *Diary: How to Improve the World (You Will Only Make Matters Worse)* (New York: Something Else Press, 2015).

15. Carol Cohn, "When Masculinity Meets Missiles," *New York Times*, January 6, 2018.

16. J. M. Coetzee, "Daniel Defoe, *Roxana*," in *Late Essays 2006–2017* (New York: Penguin Random House, 2017). "Seduction, the thought of seduction, the approach of seduction, the imagined experience of seduction, turns out to be profoundly seductive, even irresistible."

17. I came across another damning note on Joe Biden — this time with racist implications: "He described then-candidate Barack Obama in 2007 as an African-American who was 'articulate and bright and clean.' Clean? As opposed to what?"

Charles M. Blow, "Joe Biden Is Problematic on Racial Issues," *New York Times*, September 16, 2019. Forgive me, I must spell it out: Is Biden suggesting that most African-Americans are literally "dirty" or is he suggesting they are "corrupt"?

17a. "Such transgressions" are neither exceptional nor have they gone unremarked by us mortals. More out of propriety than negligence, I have yet to remind Apollo that some of our ancients, like Euripides, did not hold the gods in very high esteem. To wit: "He believed it was enough to show these gods as the legends make them — capricious, lustful, lying, outrageous in revenge, careless of honor." Mary Renault, *The Mask of Apollo* (New York: Pantheon, 1966), p. 64.

17b. Taffy Brodesser-Akner, "All That Glitters," *New York Times Magazine*, April 28, 2019, p. 26.

17c. Wil S. Hylton, "Man to Man," *New York Times Magazine*, May 12, 2019, p. 32.

18. Bret Stephens, "How Trump Could Win Next Year," *New York Times*, May 25, 2019.

18a. Elizabeth Kolbert, "Under Water: Can Engineers Save Louisiana's Disappearing Coast?", *New Yorker*, April 1, 2019, pp. 32–45.

18b. Stanley Reed, "Fusion Powers the Sun: Can It Run Your Oven?," *New York Times*, May 14, 2019.

18c. Helen MacDonald, "In Her Orbit," interview with Nathalie Cabrol, *New York Times Magazine*, March 25, 2018, p. 59.

18d. I happened on a variation of Cabrol's pessimism in a review by Tobias Grey of Robert MacFarlane's *Underland: A Deep Time Journey* (New York: W. W. Norton, 2019), in *New York Times*, May 31, 2019: "It's difficult to get a sense of the catastrophe happening immediately. There's a deferral of the problem to an unspecified future, but actually it's happening all around us now."

19. Zora Neale Hurston, *Barracoon: The Story of the Last "Black Cargo"* (New York: Amistad, 2018), reviewed by Parul Sehgal, *New York Times*, May 2, 2018.

19a. "How now, brown cow" is a phrase used in elocution teaching to demonstrate sounds of rounded vowels. The use of the phrase in teaching dates back to at least 1926. See https://en.wikipedia.org/wiki/How_now_brown_cow (last modified January 14, 2020).

19b. Joel Kovel, *White Racism: A Psychohistory* (New York: Columbia University Press, 1984), pp. xi, 32–41, 191. (Some years after the initial publication of this book [1970], Mr. Kovel renounced psychoanalysis for its "pernicious system of diagnosis dictated by professional associations and their manuals," and began describing himself as an "eco-socialist" rather than psychoanalyst. Apollo relayed this information to Jane, hoping it might assuage some of her guilt, although I must say it hasn't done much for mine. Well into the twenty-first century that book continued to be a wellspring of truth for me (YR), despite my awareness of historical objections to its main arguments, many by Kovel himself.

19c. "Roy Wilkins said somewhere that the most he could ever hope to be is a permanent recovering sexist. Is 'permanent recovering racists' the most *we* can ever be?" Intertitle in my film *Privilege* (1990); script published in *A Woman Who: Essays, Interviews, Scripts* (Baltimore: PAJ Books, Johns Hopkins University Press, 1999), p. 331.

19d. This story was reinforced when I read Julie Otsuka's powerful novel about the internment of Japanese-Americans after the bombing of Pearl Harbor in 1941: "You've been brought here for your own protection, they were told. It was all in the interest of national security. It was a matter of military necessity. It was an opportunity for them to prove their loyalty." (Otsuka, *When the Emperor Was Divine* [New York: Anchor Books, 2002], p. 70).

It is indisputable that the punishing U.S. policies of uprooting and incarcerating native-born people and those of Japanese descent during this period were not supported by any evidence of disloyalty or malfeasance. See https://en.wikipedia.org/wiki/Internment_of_Japanese_Americans (last modified January 23, 2020).

19e. A. O. Scott, "Still Confronting Dizzying Truths," review of Spike Lee's film *BlacKKKlansman*, *New York Times*, August 10, 2018.

19f. Eric Williams, *Capitalism and Slavery* (Chapel Hill: University of North Carolina Press: 1944; 1994).

19g. Stuart Hall, *The Fateful Triangle: Race, Ethnicity, Nation* (Cambridge, MA: Harvard University Press, 2017), p. 43.

19h. Harriet Jacobs, *Incidents in the Life of a Slave Girl* (New York: Dover, 2001), p. 12.

19i. ". . . whereas refusing to be a 'single being' (Fred Moten's phrase in his *Black and Blur*) resonates with my 'combination people' phrase in the intro of my book, *Other Planes of There*. This extends to gender, and to working in different fields, disciplines and forms" (Renée Green, email correspondence, April 1, 2018).

19j. And to further complicate the above: Following an early screening of Julie Dash's *Daughters of the Dust* (1991), she said, "I don't think about racism every day," in response to which I can't help wondering if she would have said that in the second decade of the twenty-first century.

19k. Thanks to artist Marianetta Porter for this story, as reported to her by her son.

19l. Terrance Hayes, *American Sonnets for My Past and Future Assassin* (New York: Penguin, 2018), reviewed by Dan Chiasson, "Sonnets and Bullets," *New Yorker*, July 2, 2018, p. 64.

19m. Vinson Cunningham, "What Are You Laughing At?" *New Yorker,* May 13, 2019, p. 32.

20. Moises Velasquez-Manoff, "Want to Be Less Racist? Move to Hawaii," *New York Times*, June 30, 2019.

21. James Baldwin, as quoted by Pankaj Mishra, "The Religion of Whiteness Becomes a Suicide Cult," *New York Times*, September 2, 2018.

21a. Margaret Rankel, "The Way to Talk to a Racist," *New York Times*, July 31, 2018.

21b. Stuart (a Brit) to the rescue(!): "Though in one sense [race] is only one of the many discourses of cultural difference in our modern history, it has a distinctiveness, a specificity, that arises because it is the one that, however unscientifically, continues to operate using the physical markers of difference *on the body* as the privileged signifiers of its regime of truth" (Hall, *The Fateful Triangle*, pp. 69–70).

21c. Ibid, p. 73. "We thus come to understand the exercise of discursive power that is required to symbolically expel difference to the far side of the universe — and the surreptitious return whereby that which has been expelled keeps coming back home to trouble the dreams of the sleeper with the terrifying internal fears, the nightmares, of having to live with difference."

21d. Ibid, p. 79. "Does the whole horrendous experience of race in the modern world come down to nothing more or less than a metaphor or a metonym of cultural difference? . . . If so, why don't we simply give up the habit, like giving up smoking?"

It took me two weeks to get through this book during a vacation in Maine, but it was well worth it! In addition, besides absorbing Benjamin's *The Storyteller* in the ensuing two weeks, I surprised myself by roaring through Julie Otsuka's *When the Emperor Was Divine* and Paul French's *Midnight in Peking*, a gripping historical whodunit set in 1937 just before the Japanese invasion.

22. "The Grand Union," an improvisational dance cooperative that evolved from my *Continuous Project-Altered Daily* (1971).

23. Previous writing about the Judson choreographers has sometimes made the mistake of suggesting there was a unified "minimalist" aesthetic prevalent in the output of the group. On the contrary, there were well over a hundred and fifty participants in those concerts who represented a wide range of sensibilities, political concerns, and performance strategies.

On a different note, we have been accused of a unified racism. Granted, we didn't reach out and try to recruit dancers of color. The Judson Dance Theater was as democratic — and anarchic — a social organism as one could imagine. All who attended its weekly workshops — dancers and non-dancers alike — could get his and her contributions performed on the official programs. The existence of the workshops was made known through word of mouth, and that their composition was mostly white was due more to the experimental and nontraditional nature of the participants' performance interests than to any lack of social or political awareness. Rudy Perez, of Puerto Rican extraction, was one of the few exceptions to the racial homogeneity during the heyday — 1962–64 — of Judson; in 1965–66 musicians Bill Dixon and Cecil Taylor performed there, as did, soon after, Suzushi Hanayagi. Although our workshops and attendant performances were not exclusionary with respect to race and ethnicity, a kind of de facto segregation was nonetheless operative, similar to so many other economic and social stratifications in the U.S. that followed on the heels of nineteenth-century slavery and the undermining of Reconstruction after the Civil War. Though not in collusion with the legacy of those forces, it can be said that our milieu was inevitably affected by them.

24. Philip Rucker and Carol Leonnig, *A Very Stable Genius*, quoted by Dwight Garner in "Comic Horror in D.C.," *New York Times*, January 21, 2020.

24a. A term I first encountered in Roger Cohen's "It's Time to Depopularize 'Populist,'" *New York Times*, July 14, 2018.

24b. Malcolm Bull, "Can the Poor Think?" *London Review of Books*, July 4, 2019, p. 3.

24c. Liu Cixin, quoted by Jiayang Fan, "The War of the Worlds," *New Yorker*, June 24, 2019, p. 29.

25. Peter Sloterdijk, *Rage and Time* (New York: Columbia University Press, 2010), quoted by Thomas Meaney, "Doktor Zeitgeist," *New Yorker*, February 26, 2018, pp. 32, 33.

26. Benjamin Carter Hett, *The Death of Democracy: Hitler's Rise to Power and the Downfall of the Weimar Republic* (New York: Henry Holt, 2018), reviewed by Alex Ross, "The Hitler Vortex: How American Racism Influenced Nazi Thought," *New Yorker*, April 30, 2018, p. 66.

27. Monica Majoli, email correspondence, July 28, 2018.

28. Tim Kreider, "Go Ahead, Millennials, Destroy Us," *New York Times*, March 3, 2018. "I just wish you could live to see the world without us."

29. Christine Murray, email correspondence, February 24, 2018.

30. Tony Kushner, *Angels in America* (New York: Theatre Communications Group, 1992).

31. Carl Zimmer, "The Secret Lives of Rodent Divas," *New York Times*, March 5, 2019.

32. Isaac Julien, *Lessons of the Hour–Frederick Douglass,* at Metro Pictures, New York, March 8–April 13, 2019.

33. Jane Goodall, interviewed by Melena Ryzik, *New York Times*, October 21, 2017.

34. Terese Marie Mailhot, *Heart Berries: A Memoir* (Berkeley: Counterpoint, 2017), reviewed by Parul Sehgal, *New York Times*, January 30, 2018.

35. Donal Ryan, *From a Low and Quiet Sea* (New York: Penguin, 2018), reviewed by Parul Sehgal, *New York Times*, August 1, 2018.

35a. A related quote hit me between the eyes: "During Ramadan, Han officials took their Uighur colleagues out to lunch and kept a list of those who abstained from eating [pork]"! Sarah A. Topol, "The Disappeared," *New York Times*, February 2, 2020.

36. Florbela Espanca, quoted by Sheila Heti in a review of Paulina Chiziane's *The First Wife*, *London Review of Books*, July 13, 2017, p. 21.

37. By now you've probably figured out — correctly — that Apollo and I read more book reviews, newspapers, and magazine articles than books. Also see more movies! He assured me, however, that he had every intention of taking a stack of books back to Olympus when he leaves Earth.

As for Apollo's ongoing account of his earthly adventures and in spite of a recurring and futile attempt at closure, I, for one, will probably continue to augment this screed where he left off, at least until our miscreant in the White House is gone.

38. Walter Benjamin, "The Second Self: A New Year's Story for Contemplation," in *The Storyteller: Tales Out of Loneliness* (New York: Verso, 2016), p. 27.

38a. Ibid., pp. 31–50.

38b. Benjamin, Thesis IX, "On the Concept of History," in *The Storyteller*, p. 207.

39. An alternate version of the last line of Renée Green's video *Begin Again, Begin Again* (2015), quoted from a poem by Paul Bowles (*Next to Nothing*, 1976): "One day my words may comfort you, as yours can never comfort me."

40. Stephen Greenblatt, *The Swerve: How the World Became Modern* (New York: W.W. Norton, 2011), p. 71.

41. In his 1927 review of *Greek Journey* (Johann Jacob Bachofen's diary of his travels in Greece in 1851), Walter Benjamin writes: "In Bachofen's mythologies, penetrating insight into the ethnological primal phenomena of the mythical is in struggle with the cavalier affirmation of the Apollonian right up into Christianity, which was probably nothing more for him than the last world-historical victory of Apollo" (*The Storyteller: Tales Out of Loneliness*, p. 142).

I have a feeling that our Sun god would be a bit miffed were he to read Benjamin's suggestion that Apollo's nineteenth-century visit to Earth resulted in a "last world-historical victory"! I must remind you of the latter's subsequent — and not always unsuccessful — visits and his assertion, as recently as last month, "I'll be back!," pronounced in no uncertain terms just before he took off for Olympus. True, given the state of things down here, Benjamin's assessment may yet prove prophetic, but meanwhile . . .

42. Jonah Raskin, *Out of the Whale: Growing Up in the American Left* (New York: Links Books, 1974), p. 211.

43. For the Irish Museum of Modern Art in Dublin (May 12, 2018), Apollo substituted: "P.S.: Just before leaving Earth, I trekked up to O'Brien's Tower atop the spectacular cliffs of Moher. You people are so fortunate: We don't have anything like that on Mount Olympus!"

44. For Apollo's Stockholm lecture (October 5, 2018), he substituted: "P.S.: Yesterday I took a ferry out to the Stockholm Archipelago. You people are so fortunate: We don't have anything like that on Mount Olympus!"

45. For his lecture at the Whitney Independent Study Program (October 18, 2018), Apollo ended with: "P.P.S.: With undying gratitude, I can assert that I would not have had the *chutzpah* to engage you in this manner without having attended a great many seminars at the ISP!"

46. Vinson Cunningham, "The Bad Place: How the Idea of Hell Has Shaped the Way We Think," *New Yorker*, January 21, 2019, p. 60.

47. *Yvonne Rainer: Dance Works*, Raven Row, London, July 11 to August 10, 2014.

48. Idrees Kahloon, "The Leveller," *New Yorker*, March 9, 2020, p. 75.

Pedagogical Vaudeville 3
by Yvonne Rainer

"Pedagogical Vaudeville 3" was a performance by Danish art students that resulted from a workshop that I conducted in Copenhagen at the invitation of Yvette Brackman, an American performance artist who was teaching at the Danish Academy of Art. A preliminary correspondence between us set the stage for the materials and ideas I would provide for the students in preparation for the final event, which took place on April 14, 2000.

What is unique about this document is that — choreographically, architecturally, and socially — it involves a process that I have never recorded in such detail as it went along, before or since! My more recent choreographic ventures, on the other hand, entail a more calculated kind of "cherry-picking" from decades of work, and are not geared to discovery each time with a new group of performers — the "Raindears," my current group, more simply, are accustomed to executing a somewhat predetermined script. There is also the difference between working with professional dancers rather than art students who had no performing experience. The latter instance creates more of a workshop than a series of professional rehearsals, with the result that in Copenhagen I felt I had to bring in "ideas" rather than predetermined moves that they for the most part would have been ill equipped to execute.

The other difference between my "professional" custom and the Copenhagen situation was the unforeseen and nontraditional nature of the Danish Academy performance space itself — i.e., the two rooms that ultimately became our unlikely base of operations — in contrast to the more conventional spaces the Raindears are used to, which create a kind of "readymade" in terms of audience positioning and framing.

Furthermore, my dance group's professionalism prompts an entirely different range of possibilities. The comparison raises questions of modern dance history in relation to "postmodern" improvisation and accident, although after Copenhagen I have cited my subsequent choreographies as examples of my own postmodernism. Ha! What passes for avant-garde for one generation is "merely modern" at another historical moment, albeit in this case, perhaps, in reverse chronological order — the earlier (Danish) performance of 2000 seeming more "avant-garde" or postmodern than the dances created in the ensuing eighteen years! It might be interesting for someone — YOU? — to use the Pedagogical Vaudeville diary as a score for an entirely new dance! Be my guest.

Preliminary email correspondence with Yvette Brackman and Karena Nomi

January 15, 2000
Dear Yvette:

It would necessarily be a quite short performance, and I would have to send instructions/assignments beforehand, such as:

Prepare a 1- to 4-minute presentation derived from 1) what you have recently or are currently reading; 2) the last movie you saw; or 3) a "situation" (invented or based on fact).

I purposely use the term "presentation" and do not specify the medium. It can be as simple as the reading of a text or as complicated as the time and place of presentation allows. One stipulation: no pantomime!

***

March 16, 2000
Dear Yvonne,

If you have already sent the Noël Carroll text to my home address it's fine and I will forward it to the students. but if you have not yet sent it please send it to the address below to the attention of Ida Pagh Davidsen, the secretary for Mur og Rum and she will distribute it to the students directly. I will also give the students copies of the scripts and Peggy Phelan's essay.

The students are meeting as a group this Monday to discuss possible areas to focus on in the workshop — a recent reading, film or event. Just to be sure do you want them to each come up with one of these areas to focus on individually or would you like for them to agree as a group?

Also, at this point I am sure that approximately 12 students are attending the workshop. Do you have a limit of students you would like to work with? We are all looking forward to your visit.

Kind regards, Yvette Brackman

***

March 16, 2000
Dear Yvette:

I am sending the Noël Carroll text to the school, attention of Ida Pagh Davidsen. In answer to your questions:

To avoid a bunch of solo "acts" each student should—individually—think about how many people he or she wants as part of her/his presentation and enlist the necessary cooperation. Any one of these could conceivably be a solo or involve as many as the whole group. No single presentation—by individual or individuals—should be more than three minutes. I think 15 people is the maximum number of participants. So there is the potential for 15 presentations. The medium is up to them: live/recorded speech, live action, video, film, discussion, recitation, reading, description of yet-to-be realized presentation. More than one presentation can happen at a time.

I must constantly remind myself of the value of mistakes, failures, interruptions, breakdowns, interferences, accidents, incompletions, muddles, mix-ups . . . and chance occurrences. They don't have to totally organize everything. They don't have to reveal everything to each other. They can surprise each other . . . and me. Have fun.

***

Copenhagen, 27 March
Dear Yvonne Rainer:
We (the students) have had a meeting to prepare for your workshop.

We discussed what a title/theme for the workshop could be—and decided to present you with an idea we already are working with in connection with a workshop we are "teaching" in May—The (inventing of) everyday rituals that have to do with the idea of "the good life."

There have been several interpretations of the instructions/ assignments you sent for us to prepare. Do you want each of us to prepare a presentation as you described—derived from a common theme as the one we suggest above—or are you interested in a more individual "inspiration" . . . or is it for us to decide?

We are meeting again on Friday 31 of March—so if you have any comments, I would be glad to hear from you.

Kind Regards, Karena Nomi

***

March 27, 2000

Dear Karena Nomi:

The problem with a "common theme" is that it runs the risk of propelling your work as a group into conventional structures of development and resolution. It is easier to fall into this trap than you may think. I myself am more interested in heterogeneity than homogeneity. But "the good life" sounds like a terrific idea. What is it, who is offering it, what are our expectations of it, how is desire organized, expressed, or, as the case may be, suppressed? I think, therefore I shop (to paraphrase Barbara Kruger). Etc., etc. What is "the bad life?" What are you reading?

As for methods of working, can you think along the lines of how each of you, individually, want to use anywhere from one to 15 people in any single presentation or segment? One factor may be the social composition of the group. Do you all know each other? Have you worked with each other before? Would someone prefer to be behind a video camera to document your discussions, which in turn might constitute a segment of the whole, or might provide a "template" from which you could "re-enact" parts of discussions? These are my free-association ramblings. Use them as you see fit.

And keep in touch.

Best, Yvonne—I look forward to meeting all of you.

#

SUNDAY

Karena Nomi meets me at the airport and takes me by taxi to the hotel several blocks from the Academy. In response to my questions, she tells me she has studied ballet and modern dance before enrolling at the Academy. She points out various sights, most interesting is Christiana, the former naval base that has been a squatters' settlement since the early '70s. I crash for several hours, then prepare to meet Yvette Brackman and Amy Sillman for dinner. Amy, a very talented painter whose exhibition I have just seen in New York and immensely liked, has been teaching here for a week and will stay on for another week. I am looking forward to seeing her in this context. There is a knock at my door. It is Amy, in all her usual exuberance. The three of us have dinner near the harbor. Yvette is the recently appointed American director of the "Mur og Rum" ("Walls and Spaces") School, an autonomous entity within the Academy. She explains the workings and structure of the Academy. I describe my correspondence and taxi ride with Karena. Yvette tells me that Karena, who is a first-year student, had been accepted on the basis of her art submission, a large blue-screen blue cube. We marvel at the gutsiness of a dancer to make such a bold move.

Amy suggests a collaboration. She has assigned her painting students the task of making large painted balls, about a yard in diameter. Could they be used in the performance? I immediately pounce on the idea of having them rolled into the space during the show. Both Yvette and Amy smoke after dinner. It's been a long time since I was last exposed to European smoking culture. No repairing to the bar area in this neck of the world. Later that night my jet-lag keeps me awake for several hours. I make the following jottings on individual slips of paper from a note-pad:

> Move as slowly as you can throughout this session.
> Measure the room with your body.
> Define "happening."
> Define "modern dance."
> Describe a scene from a movie that impressed you.
> Execute unaccustomed activities with a chair.
> Describe a walk in the city.
> In rapid succession, perform static poses that express or are in response to the following:
>> I am in despair.
>> I love you.
>> Why don't you love me?
>> Why are you abusing me?

I am enraged at you.
You abandoned me!
Why did you leave me?
I'm gay.
I thought you'd never come.
I long for you.
I'm scared.
Don't be scared.
I am overjoyed.

Make a list of gestures as you observe them during the first session, then perform them in the same order.

MONDAY

We convene in a large room off a cobble-stoned courtyard which is enclosed on four sides by the imposing facades of an eighteenth-century palace. As the students arrive, I give each of them one of the slips of paper.

Yvette has already informed me that the workshop will take place elsewhere. When everyone–at this point, nine women and two men–has arrived, we walk across the courtyard, splitting halfway into two groups. One group has moved toward the main gate, another toward a side door. Thinking I am walking in the wrong direction, I change course and follow on the heels of the group walking toward the main entrance. Others do the same until someone, probably Yvette, tells us to go toward "the door." We reverse direction and straggle into the building through the correct entrance, then up several flights of stairs, down a long hallway into the first and larger of two connecting and almost empty rooms. The floors are the original eighteenth-century wide planks and resound to our steps with a hearty clatter. Adjacent to the larger room is an even larger auditorium filled to capacity with rows of chairs. Yvette tells me we will be able to perform in the auditorium. I begin to imagine the main performance taking place in there, with sounds emanating from the rooms adjacent to it, which, as of this writing, I shall refer to as rooms #1 and #2.

But for the time being we shall work in rooms #1 and #2 and not in the chair-clotted auditorium. We clear some wooden slats from room #1 and put them in a storage area across the corridor. (Later, when I have a fleeting urge to recover this material and repeat the action of "clearing" it, I find the storage room locked. By the time the caretaker unlocks this room several days later, I will have forgotten the original reason for my request.)

I suggest we enter room #1 from the auditorium and walk in the same patterns as we did in the courtyard. After doing that, I ask them to run in the same patterns. Following this, we pause near the doorway to room #2. I say, "Why don't we try doing the same thing in the other room?" We run into room #2 and execute the same patterns. I ask them to go back to room #1 and recreate the dialogue that had taken place just before the last maneuver, to be preceded by my "Why don't we . . ." (Marie asks Maria from Malmö what group she was in. Maria from Malmö replies something like, "I was going toward the toilet." Marie says, "Then you should be with us." Maria accordingly moves over. We all then run into room #2.)

Siemi performs her presentation, which she had prepared prior to my arrival, a combination of moving and speaking. It is very polished. Her experience and professionalism are very apparent and dominate my impression. We talk about that for a bit. I am concerned already about how to integrate different levels of performing experience into a whole. (Yvette, as it turns out, is especially concerned about this with regard to Siemi.) In the afternoon Siemi performs the sequence of gestures she had observed in the morning. Her style is percussive and dance-like, not at all like everyday gestures. I ask her to soften her movement. She says "sloppy" and repeats the sequence. I express approval and ask, "Did that feel sloppy?" She says, "No." I am aware of imposing my bias, but feel justified, given the time constraint of four and a half days in which to come up with something I can call a "performance." If Siemi's style sets the standard, the others will be at a disadvantage. Easier (and far preferable from my point of view) to expand Siemi's horizons than to drill the others in some kind of dancerly performance mode.

I give a rudimentary explanation of my interest in "ordinary" movement, how people are not accustomed to thinking about it as performance, how our expectations as audience are usually geared toward some kind of transformation, how potential performers such as themselves can begin to see their untrained physicality as a resource. I stress the importance for someone of Siemi's experience to challenge and expand her habitual ways of doing things.

Karena presents her "staring piece." It begins with Rega seated behind a table staring at five others facing her in a row about four feet from the table. After several minutes four leave and place their chairs on either side of Rega. There are now five people behind the table staring at Maria from Malmö, who has remained in place. The first loner can be seen as some kind of authority figure or judge appraising a group of supplicants. The second solitary figure becomes a criminal being judged by a jury. The relation of chairs to table is the deciding factor.

Elsebeth has brought in string and instruction books for the whole group with which to play Cat's Cradle. We all pair off and try to do it. I suggest

Elsebeth play it with Marie, who has the assignment of describing a "walk in the city." The two activities can occur simultaneously.

I notice that Orse, an extremely shy Hungarian woman who speaks and understands hardly any English, has taken her assignment very seriously and has been moving around the room in slow motion regardless of what the others are doing. I start laughing and have to admit that I had entirely forgotten that I had given her that slip of paper.

I try to stage all of the assignments that have been carried out. Anders's contribution is to sit cross-legged on the floor, drawing in a self-absorbed way on a pad of paper. He has already shown signs of discontent. What is taking place here is apparently not what he expected. Nevertheless, I stow his activity in my mental archive as something potentially useful.

As we are ending the session, I catch Jens and Anders doing some pugilistic fooling around and suggest that the two of them work out the assignment of "Emotional Gestures" (which will eventually become "Romantic Trio").

Yvette, Amy, and I again have dinner together. When I get back to the hotel I notice that my clothes reek from the day's and evening's accumulation of smoke. I must stifle my horror that all of my students, most of them in their early twenties, are avid smokers.

TUESDAY

I learn from the concierge that the auditorium is barred to us because of the fragility of the mural on the ceiling of the room below. I resign myself to working and performing in the two smaller spaces. I report this to the group. Michelle suggests that, weather permitting, we could do the performance outside. I immediately veto that suggestion without explaining why. A reflex dictated by the lack of time to transpose material from one space to a totally different one. We have fewer than five days. (It doesn't occur to me until Michelle reminds me two days later over drinks that my response was discomfitingly abrupt.)

Arthur shows up for the first time. I give him the assignment of defining "happening." Siemi informs me that due to a prior commitment she may not be able to be present on Friday, the day of the performance, but she would like to attend until then. I ask her to teach everyone her sequence of gestures, also to add to it. We all stand in a circle and practice and add to the sequence of pedestrian moves. One of them is a habitual gesture of Yvette's, who happens to be present while we are working on this exercise. She enters the process with good-natured humor, allowing the group to appropriate this token of her hitherto unselfconscious dailiness.

Clasp hands behind head.
Do "Yvette's" parallel forearms to right.
Look over left shoulder, look straight ahead.
Lean hands on knees, look right, then left.
Straighten up while right hand wipes mouth with sniff.
Brush dust off thighs.
Scratch neck with left hand.
Brush hair back with right hand.
Exhale with a loud "Ha!"
Lift right hip and leg to side.
Shake left hand at arm's length beside thigh.

Marie contributes a card game involving four people. I file this away as a suitable event to follow the running. The concentration demanded by the task immediately eliminates the possibility of self-consciousness.

We look at various people's execution of their assignments.

Anders seems to have dropped out. I assign the "Emotional Gestures" to Jens and Karena. There is much hilarity as they work up the sequence while the rest of us watch.

I add further assignments:

Bring in a text dealing with sex, race, or class. Think about ways of presenting it not only as a straight reading.
Bring in an object and devise a group activity around it.
Think about sound or music that can accompany the activities.

WEDNESDAY

People show their objects. We are all nonplussed by Karena's plaster bell pepper and red feather boa, Jens's passport, a fetish-like thing wrapped in blue plastic twine, some seashells, a brick. Arthur's black rubber-wrapped megaphone is the only object that suggests immediate use. He will speak his rap about happenings through it.

Long-haired Maria announces she would prefer to be a spectator rather than a performer. I ask her why. She is unclear about her reason. I don't argue, and she sits on the sidelines.

I have decided that the audience will at first be stationed in room #1 and the opening maneuver of the "Vaudeville" will be the surging of the whole group into room #1 from room #2, followed by the pause and regrouping with discussion before running back into room #2. The activities that will follow the running and be performed simultaneously in room #1 have begun to accumulate:

1) The card players; 2) Orse walks and gestures in slow motion; 3) Rega walks back and forth talking about modern dance; 4) Maria from Malmö does various things with a chair and string; 5) Marie describes a walk in the city while doing Cat's Cradle with Elsebeth; 6) Arthur talks about happenings. A miniature Tower of Babel.

The card game involves feats of memory. About three dozen cards with photos of Japanese cuisine on one side are spread face down in a grid pattern. Each player has two turns turning over cards. The object is to remember the exact placement of a given card and try to match it with its double. The players had been Jens, Michelle, Rega, and long-haired Maria, but now Maria has dropped out. As we are discussing whether to do it with three people or appoint a fourth, long-haired Maria changes her mind and says she will participate. I give her an ultimatum: "You're either in or out. Make up your mind." She says she has been "silly," that there's no good reason for her to be a spectator. I don't say it, but I hope she has a better reason to be a participant.

I am entranced by Orse's dreamy walking. She ever so slowly brings her hands to her face and down again as she walks. Maria from Malmö rolls her chair around, ties it to a pipe, talks softly to it, strokes it as though it is a pet.

Arthur contributes a CD of a black rap group that he wants to try out with the card game. We play it and are startled at the contrast between the ghetto lyrics and the blond Nordic card players. He thinks – and I agree – the two should go together.

Karena reports she would like to try out an audio tape of a cat purring to accompany her "Staring Piece." The trouble is, it's on a DAT, and Michelle's recorder, which we have been using, plays only CDs or regular cassettes. Michelle offers to transfer the DAT to a cassette.

Marie, Karena, Michelle, and Rega have brought texts, seemingly without a clue as to how to stage them. Rega reads from Henry Miller. I suggest she climb up and down a tall ladder that had been left in room #2. It is a very lovely performance. Looking like a tiny sprite, she hikes up her long skirt and carefully picks her way up and over the top and down the other side while reading in a delicate wavering voice. Somehow Elsebeth gets into an argument with her. Elsebeth hates Henry Miller, while Rega loves the writing. I ask if they can conduct the argument while climbing up and down the ladder. They at first balk, feel that their arguing is too private an activity. Finally they agree on Rega reading and when she pauses Elsebeth will intervene with several sentences, like "Henry Miller makes me feel like a victim."

In Danish, Karena reads something by a newspaper columnist that is somewhat anti-feminist. When she has roughly translated it for my benefit and indicated its bias, I ask, "What can you do to show that you don't agree with him?" Marie and Maria from Malmö then work out a succession of moves that consists of toppling Karena over in her chair and manipulating her body as she continues to read, finally walking her into a wall and leaving her there.

We discuss what language the performance should be conducted in. Two of the texts brought in are in English; others are Danish newspaper clippings. It seems best not to translate the original language of each text, and whatever other speech takes place should be in Danish, or, if I am involved, in English.

Marie has devised some simple moves to accompany her reading of a news report about immigrants and unemployment. It is a concise and economical performance, taking her in four stages from sitting on the floor to sitting in a chair and underscoring different parts of her text.

I teach several of my standard configurations: "L'Enforme" and "Clump." I insert Michelle's reading (in English) of a sociological text about Danish identity into "Clump."

In the afternoon we meet in the media room, where Jens and Rega show videotapes. Rega's tape is a loop of jump-cuts of Elizabeth Taylor's "breathing moments" in *Who's Afraid of Virginia Woolf?* I ask her what she would like to do with the tape, wheel it around as it plays on a monitor, for instance. She says what she's really interested in is the inhalations. I suggest we as a group do them in quick succession. The exercise proves very effective: the intake of breath moves from one to another, then in the next round is exhaled, to be inhaled once more, etc. Someone suggests we do it as a "clump." It breaks us all up. Somehow, the initial tension in the group is broken in this ridiculously forced physical proximity with one another while breathing. We return to the original sequential breathing while sitting and standing around the table. Long-haired Maria suggests reading her text, a list of women astronomers, after several rounds of breathing and while the group breathing continues. We all agree this is a successful combination of sound and image.

Jens's tape shows him in front of a building, bellowing behind a mask, "I am alone. Who is there?" etc., and somersaulting down a hill. I ask him if he knows of Samuel Beckett. He doesn't. I explain why I've made this association and suggest he perform the mask part of the video in the first section in room #1.

THURSDAY

Andrea shows up for the first time. She has just returned from New York. I am at first doubtful that she can be integrated into the piece at this late date. She is game for whatever she can pick up and begins by learning Siemi's gesture sequence, which we again practice.

Marie reports that after talking it over at lunch the previous day, they thought it might be a good idea to just choose the activities freely in performance. I gulp and resist my impulse to "just say no." I explain that it is a matter of expediency to predetermine the order of the program. It would take much longer than the time available to us to work out all the possibilities of transition between group and individual activities if we were to use "spontaneous determination" in the performance itself. Without working out the details beforehand, their "freedom" might result in a mess. Better to know what we are doing. To handle things like freedom and indeterminacy well requires experience and time. What I don't say is that I'm the one with the most experience here and that they should trust me. There is a certain paradox here that will emerge the next day.

Karena tries out her "Staring Piece" with the "purring" tape Michelle has transferred. It is an odd combination, both sound and image singularly charged. Karena is pleased. I think it's a hit. I seem to remember I said as much.

I teach "Line with Objects." The incongruous collection now finds its place. The brick, bell pepper, newspaper, book, and a feather from Karena's boa are the objects ultimately used, passed from hand to hand as the line continually reconfigures itself. A problem arises: Where to keep the objects before they are needed? After much debate (and a bit of mock frustrated groaning on my part) Michelle suggests they be put in a basket which I will carry and from which I will distribute them during "L'Enforme."

We start to run through the entire sequence of events, which I had tentatively organized the previous night. Afterwards there are suggestions for changes. Jens doesn't feel right about his mask bit, and others remark that it doesn't fit, that it's too sentimental for this context. I am pleased that by this point there is a consensus about "fitness." They have a good sense of where the piece seems to be heading. I suggest he read his text–a news clipping about Bill Gates–while holding the mask to his face. But his mask is opaque. What to do? Michelle again comes to the rescue. She will bring a transparent plastic bowl that can serve as a mask and through which Jens will be able to read the clipping.

Arthur is tired of talking about happenings. "Could I sing a song?" He ends up singing "La Paloma" in German out of the open window through his megaphone. He is very striking in an S&M way with his jet-black hair, black shirt, and black leather pants. (I learn he is Austrian, a sword swallower, and does "vomit performances" with a partner.)

I suggest that Jens and Arthur do a gay version of "Emotional Gestures." Again there is much hilarity as they work. There follows a discussion about how to integrate the two versions, the gay and the straight. Various strategies are tried. Finally someone suggests that Jens remain in the middle and after completing the sequence with Arthur, he should turn to Karena and do it with her. This version is approved by all. And slow sleepy Jens is pleased because the strain of doing most of it on one knee (to which he descends to express the initial "I love you") will be shared by both knees. They will keep repeating the sequence until the group doing "L'Enforme" moves from room #2 into room #1.

I add a Dada bit for the opening collage in room #1: Karena and I walk toward each other on the diagonal. YR: "Where is the post office?" Karena: "What's that to me?" I exit through the door, and Karena goes to the corner.

We work on the logistics of transitions. Yvette is the guardian of the tape recorder, which will have to be moved from room #1 to room #2. In room #1, Yvette will turn it on and off. In room #2, Karena will take care of it.

FRIDAY

Amy and her painting students arrive with nine painted balls they have been working on for the last week. Yvette will roll them into either of the two rooms at irregularly spaced intervals throughout the performance. The performers and audience will simply have to move them aside or keep out of their way. There is some discussion as to how fragile the balls are. They are large balloons that had first been covered in papier-mâché, then painted in decorative and figurative patterns. In transit to our part of the building, some of them seem to have deflated a bit.

Orse and Andrea have not shown up. Yvette asks me if I'm nervous. I reply that I'm not nervous, I'm pissed off.

We start to rehearse without them. Arthur thinks that the two readings by Karena and Marie should be broken up by something else. I teach him a Futurist bit: Man enters room in an overcoat. . . . Jens lends Arthur his overcoat, and after several forays in which he breaks up laughing, Arthur does a superb agitated entrance looking at the passport he has found in the pocket, then goes to a window, turns, sees the audience, shouts, "I have no idea why I'm here!" and leaves. Jens and Karena will then follow him out to begin "Emotional Gestures" ("Romantic Trio") in room #1.

There are still glitches in the transitions. I ask them if they want another rehearsal. They are unanimous. We agree to break for lunch and reconvene at 1:00 and be through in time for the 3 p.m. performance.

After lunch, everyone assembles on time, including Orse and Andrea. (Orse had problems with her young daughter that morning; the child had smeared her face with colored inks from laundry markers just before leaving for day-care.) All the kinks are worked out. At one point in my somewhat autocratic efforts to marshal the attention of the group, Arthur reminds me – in an affectionate manner – of the preliminary email I had sent to them before arriving, in which I exhorted them to "keep in mind the value of mistakes, failures, interruptions, breakdowns, interferences, accidents, incompletions, muddles, mix-ups . . . and chance occurrences." There is no time to do anything but laugh.

Later, however, I think of what I could have said: that this statement refers to the *process* of making something, not only to its realization. There was the "accident" of the courtyard "muddle" and "mix-up"; the "interferences" of the simultaneous talking; the "chance occurrence" of the way the balls entered the spaces; the "interruption" of the Dada encounter; the "mistakes" engendered by having to read a text while doing "Clump," etc., etc.

Amy arrives and is jubilant that the balls have regained their original fullness. Everyone is alert and excited. I relax. An overflow crowd begins to gather in room #1. At 3:15 p.m. we begin. The performance lasts about a half-hour and everything goes smoothly.

#

AFTERWORD

Email Correspondence with Steve Paxton

April 25, 2000
Dear Yvonne:

. . . In your journal you definitely passed with flying colors that always awkward moment with a group when they start wanting to resort to anarchy and improvisation, to slip the traces which they have paid to import. It is a bit different from CPAD [*Continuous Project-Altered Daily*, a dance work by Y.R., 1969–1970, which eventually morphed into the improvisation-based group "Grand Union"], I think, in that we took a year's transition, but it is of a sort.

As you retained the reins in this event, what is your assessment of it? It sounds to me like you managed to collect much of the extrania in the process into the show, nimble and focused.

And, what is the physical posture for "I am gay"?

***

April 25, 2000
Dear Steve:
Yes, it's a very precarious line I tread when I go into these situations and know but don't fully reveal to them, at least at the beginning, the degree to which I shall be holding the reins. In the two previous situations — NYU and Chicago — because of more extended time, I gave them a lot more to work with, like all kinds of films and readings from which they extrapolated performance ideas. But in Denmark I had them read, prior to my arrival, several essays on my own work [by Peggy Phelan and Noël Carroll], and when I got there I showed several of my films and did my standard lecture "Out of a Corner of the 60s," which encompasses a smattering of Cage, Cunningham, and happenings, but is mainly about Judson. All as introduciton to certain ideas. Then it was like pulling teeth or rabbits out of a hat or ideas out of a kind of Y.R. geist. They were finally very appreciative and exhilarated, as was much of the audience response, and there were no real rebellions. Probably because once the ball got rolling it was very clear that I was open to concrete suggestions and not to vague fantasies of "freedom."

To express "I am gay," Jens, a large, sleepy, slow student who did much of the exercise on one knee (to which he initially repaired to express "I love you") simply turned his head from his "Why did you leave me?" posture and looked at his partner. Nothing special, but effective nonetheless.

Email Correspondence from Gregg Bordowitz

April 27, 2000
Dear Why,

. . . One of the most exciting things about your teaching process is the way you incorporate material generated from the classroom experience immediately into the developing "text" of the class. I love reading how the performances unfold out of each other, kind of like a complicated origami figure unfolded, then refolded into something even more wonderfully complex. . . .

Finally, I would love to read your thoughts on why pedestrian, everyday movement is more compelling to you than the studied, refined and/or confident movements of dancers and performers. This has been an important issue for you throughout your career. It's an important part of your filmmaking. Why does it remain so? How has your thinking on this changed over the years? Has it changed? Why do teaching situations bring up the issue of everyday movement for you with fresh intensity?

Yvonne Rainer interviewed by Douglas Crimp, October 4, 2012

DOUGLAS CRIMP: Let's start with your dance *Assisted Living: Do You Have Any Money?* The six dancers recite a variety of lengthy texts, including jokes, newspaper stories, and film monologues, while performing complicated combinations of steps. When I saw the work in rehearsal, I found it difficult to follow the words and movement at the same time, so I can't imagine how anyone can actually perform them together.

RAINER: Well, it's a whole new challenge for my dancers. I didn't know whether they could do it, and they were kind of dubious, but it turns out they *can* do it. My dancers are not trained actors, but there are techniques. I guess from the spectator's perspective it involves a kind of de-centering, a splitting of focus—like not being able to take in everything onstage in a Cunningham dance when different things are happening at the same time. The dance events in *Assisted Living: Do You Have Any Money?* all happen as unison duets or trios, so I hope that the doubling and tripling of the movement makes it a bit easier to focus on the speech. I don't expect you to follow the monologues in their entirety. But you can get the gist, or go back and forth with your attention. Of course, a second viewing makes the process easier. But anyway, the aesthetic of it is very strange. I don't know quite how to talk about it yet. First of all, the dance is set up in a carnivalesque way, with me being rolled in, sitting in a big, overstuffed chair. I stand up in it and read a text like a carnival barker trying to con his audience into seeing the freak show: "Step right up, folks . . ." There's a basic step that I worked out with them, which has its origin in a solo I made in the mid-'60s called *At My Body's House*—what we call the *petit pas*,

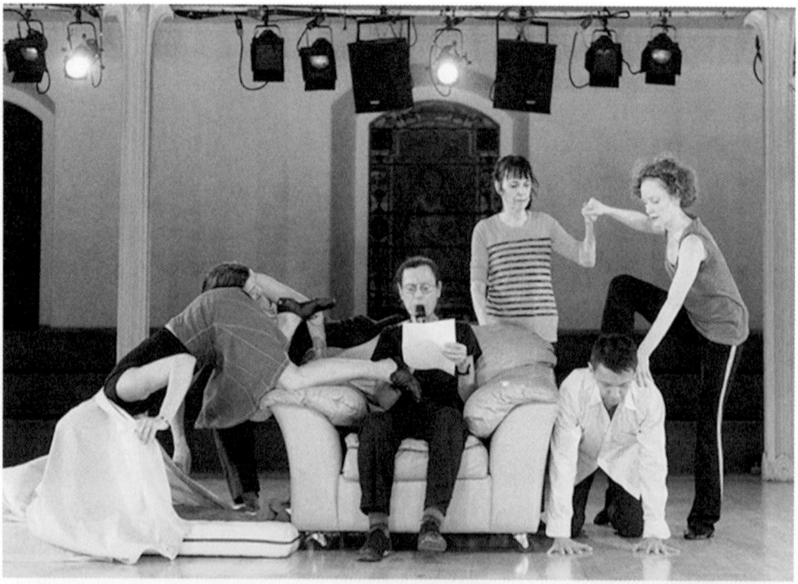

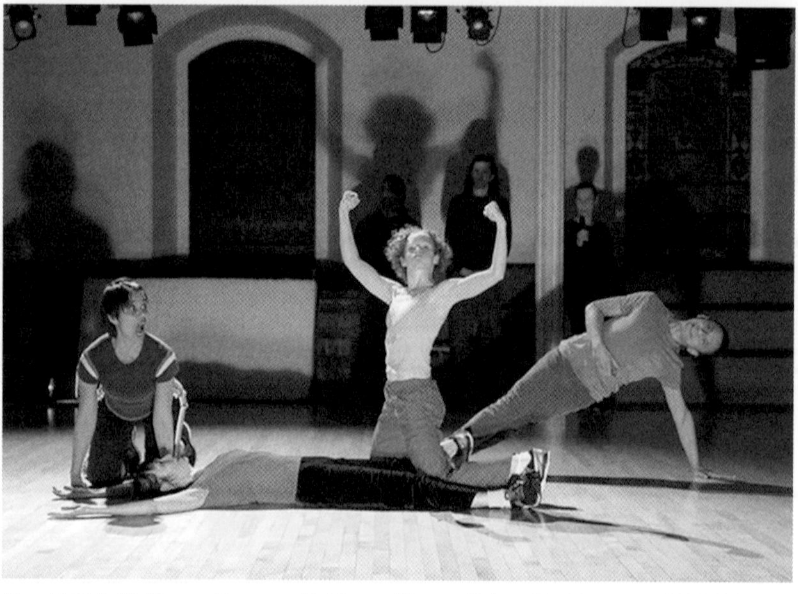

Top: Patricia Hoffbauer, Emmanuelle Phuon, Yvonne Rainer, Pat Catterson, Keith Sabado, and Emily Coates in *Assisted Living: Do You Have Any Money?*, 2013.
Bottom: Emmanuelle Phuon, Pat Catterson, Emily Coates, and Keith Sabado in *Assisted Living: Good Sports* 2, 2011. Both performed at Danspace, New York, 2013.

which is a series of simple dance steps that they do in unison at the very beginning. After that, most of the dancing comes from Laurel and Hardy shorts. There's also a ballet adagio that Emily Coates and Keith Sabado do that Keith was first using to warm up the dancers, an academic exercise with arabesques and développés. While the two of them are doing the adagio, Keith recites an academic description of Keynesian economics, so there are these two kinds of academic things going on at one time from two different traditions, one from ballet and one from economics.

CRIMP: Keynes was married to a ballerina.

RAINER: Keynes? But I thought he was gay.

CRIMP: He was, and he was also a balletomane. He married Lydia Lopokova, one of the stars of Diaghilev's Ballets Russes.

RAINER: Hmm . . . So, that's one of the first combinations of texts and dances. And so it goes. There's a quote from Emma Goldman.

CRIMP: And there's Eric Emerson's monologue from *The Chelsea Girls* (1966), which you found in my book on Andy Warhol's films. Are all of the texts appropriated?

RAINER: Yes. I didn't write any of the texts.

CRIMP: And the movement, too, is mostly taken from elsewhere.

RAINER: Yes. Except for the *petit pas*, it's all taken from elsewhere.

CRIMP: You spoke while dancing your very first dance—*Three Satie Spoons*, from 1960—saying, for example, "The grass is greener when the sun is yellower." And you've continued to use spoken language in many of your dances. When you did *Three Satie Spoons*, had you heard anyone else use the spoken word in a dance? What made you think you could get away with it?

RAINER: I certainly was not the first to do it. From what I understand, some of Merce Cunningham's early solos had speaking in them.

CRIMP: Yes, I was thinking of Cunningham's *How to Pass, Kick, Fall, and Run*, in which John Cage recites stories while the company dances. But that was later, in 1965.

RAINER: Yeah. But the dancers don't speak. That's a whole other ballgame. Also, I'm interested in the idea of "radical juxtaposition," a term coined by Susan Sontag to describe Happenings, putting two things next to each other, or one after the other, that don't have any obvious connection. I think it can be used to characterize all of my work in both dance and film.

CRIMP: It's interesting that in your best-known work, *Trio A* from 1966, you don't use language.

RAINER: Ah, that's not true! I don't think you saw me doing it at Judson two years ago—it's probably the last time I will ever do it, because it gets harder and harder for me to do. While dancing, I spoke about the difficulty of doing it at my age—which, it turned out, produced a laugh riot. I would say, "This is supposed to be a slow rise of the leg. Why can't I get my leg up higher than this now?" And then, "Oh, just do it and get it over with." There were two performances, and I even talked during the first performance about being in a state of extreme stage fright because I hadn't performed for a while.

CRIMP: But that isn't how most people would know *Trio A*. It's known as a work that doesn't have that quality of radical juxtaposition, except, perhaps, for the fact that each of the three dancers does it at his or her own pace, so they go in and out of sync. The first time you did it, at the Judson Church, you had wooden slats thrown down from the balcony onto the dance floor at regular intervals throughout the performance. So I guess that's a radical juxtaposition of sorts. Another phrase you've used more recently to describe your work is "pedagogical vaudeville."

RAINER: Yeah. In the recent work, I think that applies.

CRIMP: Perhaps one could also think of *Trio A* as having a certain pedagogical value. It shows us, by the omission of phrasing, how much we depend on the attack, arrest, and recovery of traditional dance phrasing to be able to locate a dance's meaning, or to be able to see a dance at all.

RAINER: Yeah, you might also say that *Trio A* is a kind of lexicon of movement possibilities.

CRIMP: You were just saying that when you recently danced *Trio A*, people saw it as a laugh riot, but your funny side is very often overlooked. Your work is often seen as overly intellectual, maybe because you're known as the theoretician of Judson, and because in your films you often took on serious political topics—class privilege, rape, cancer, racism, the battle of the sexes. People focus more on the pedagogy and less on the vaudeville.

RAINER: Right, I don't know why. Perhaps because of my association with Minimalism. In the standard view, Judson Dance is seen as part of Minimalism. I hope this Danspace series will disabuse people of that notion. You know, my work at Judson was very eclectic, and the participants at Judson came from very diverse backgrounds, training, and disciplines. But the pervasive view of Judson is of me and Steve Paxton walking and running.

CRIMP: "Ordinary movement" became the catchall idea associated with Judson.

RAINER: It's true that I explored so-called pedestrian movement, but it's always been in relation to other kinds of movement. My work requires trained dancers.

CRIMP: Although there are early pieces, like *We Shall Run* (1963), that could be done by untrained dancers.

RAINER: Well, that is an example of a more minimal piece. But, even though the only movement in that piece is trotting around, I juxtaposed that movement with a very dramatic section of the Berlioz Requiem. So I was always interested in mixing it up.

CRIMP: I wish people would pay more attention to the vaudevillian aspects of your work. Even the "one thing after another" aspect of Minimalism provided you a structure of radical juxtaposition in the late 1960s—pieces you called Performance Demonstrations, Composites, or Fractions, in which unrelated events followed one after another but didn't necessarily seem to have much to do with one another. They had very much the character of vaudeville, where a ballet pas de deux might be followed by a trained seal act or a juggler. In fact, you did put a juggler on-stage with your dancers in *The Mind Is a Muscle* in 1968. And you've also done a lot of things, like, say, *Chair/Pillow* from *Continuous Project – Altered Daily*, in 1970, in which a group of dancers performs an on-the-beat routine with folding chairs and pillows to Ike and Tina Turner's "River Deep, Mountain High." It often brings people to their feet.

RAINER: Yeah, *Chair/Pillow* is a crowd-pleaser.

CRIMP: This goofball-entertainer side of you interests me, especially in relation to your lifelong commitment to the avant-garde. You speak very movingly of this in your interview with Gregg Bordowitz that is the centerpiece of *Rainer Variations*, your collaborative video with Charles Atlas. And, of course, one of the great pedagogical vaudevillian moments of that video is your attempt to teach *Trio A* to Richard Move in the guise of Martha Graham. I'd be interested to hear you talk about the relation between the side of you that is a bit of a ham and the side that is so fundamentally serious, politically engaged, pedagogical, avant-garde. How do these things work together for you?

RAINER: I'm interested in how they *don't* work, putting things together that don't fit. You know, vaudeville and pratfalls and slapstick don't fit with, uh, what's going on in Syria now. Not that I would put those two things in a dance, but my daily life—, I'm a news junkie, and my daily life is so infused with reports of atrocity. It makes me feel helpless and demoralized, what leaders of the world perpetuate—it's horrific. And I have to get my response to it into my work in some way. Like in the earlier *Assisted Living* piece—*Assisted Living: Good Sports 2*. Toward the end, the dancers are lying on the floor with their heads on each other's bellies, laughing their heads off, and I go toward them holding a microphone and say, "Have you heard the one about Steve Jobs and the Chinese iPhone factory worker who had half his face blown off? They go into a bar, see, and . . ." I riff on this impossible situation. I had just been reading in the paper about the conditions in the iPhone factories in China. And we're all complicit and helpless in these technological advances and hysterical marketing of devices that we must have in order to go on with our lives. They have us by the short hairs. My audiences are all primed in the same way—they read the papers, too. I know I'm delivering these missals to the already persuaded. But it's an attempt to keep up a kind of recognition and . . . not guilt, but awareness and mutual support, you know?

CRIMP: The technique of radical juxtaposition makes it possible for you to do it, and it makes it perfectly continuous with what you've been doing all along. But it also brings the audience up short. You're going along enjoying the dance, and suddenly you're confronted with something like this, and you think, "What do I do with this? What sort of response can I have to this?" So this pedagogical vaudeville has a genuine aesthetic function. It's not just a way for *you* to cope. It's a way to make a dance solicit a much more complex response. I think of what dance critic Deborah Jowitt wrote about the sentence you give to Pat Catterson in *Assisted Living: Good Sports 2*, "Oh frontal lobes: Who needs 'em?" to which the audience generally laughs: "But would that be the frontal lobes whose function Wikipedia defines as the ability 'to recognize future consequences resulting from current actions, to choose between good and bad actions…'?"

RAINER: I have developed a morbid fascination with Mitt Romney during the election campaign. This is a new kind of person, someone who deals only in the abstractions of money, private equity firms that deal in algorithms of finance and profit. It's a new kind of capitalist, very different from the old guys who owned factories that made things. This is a whole new ballgame, and the irony is that Romney cannot possibly talk about this in his campaign because no one understands it. Probably even he doesn't understand the half of it. This culture of money is changing all our lives in ways that we can't even calibrate.

CRIMP: I'm thinking back to an earlier moment when you responded to a political issue in your work, when you did *Trio A With Flags* for the People's Flag Show at Judson.

RAINER: Yes, the People's Flag Show was organized to protest the prosecution of Stephen Radich, a gallerist who had shown a sculpture that allegedly desecrated the flag. It was a huge show in the sanctuary of Judson Church. Jasper Johns had something in it, Kate Millett—anyone who did anything involving the flag was invited to contribute. So five of us who knew *Trio A* took off our clothes and tied five-foot flags around our necks and draped them in front of us, and we

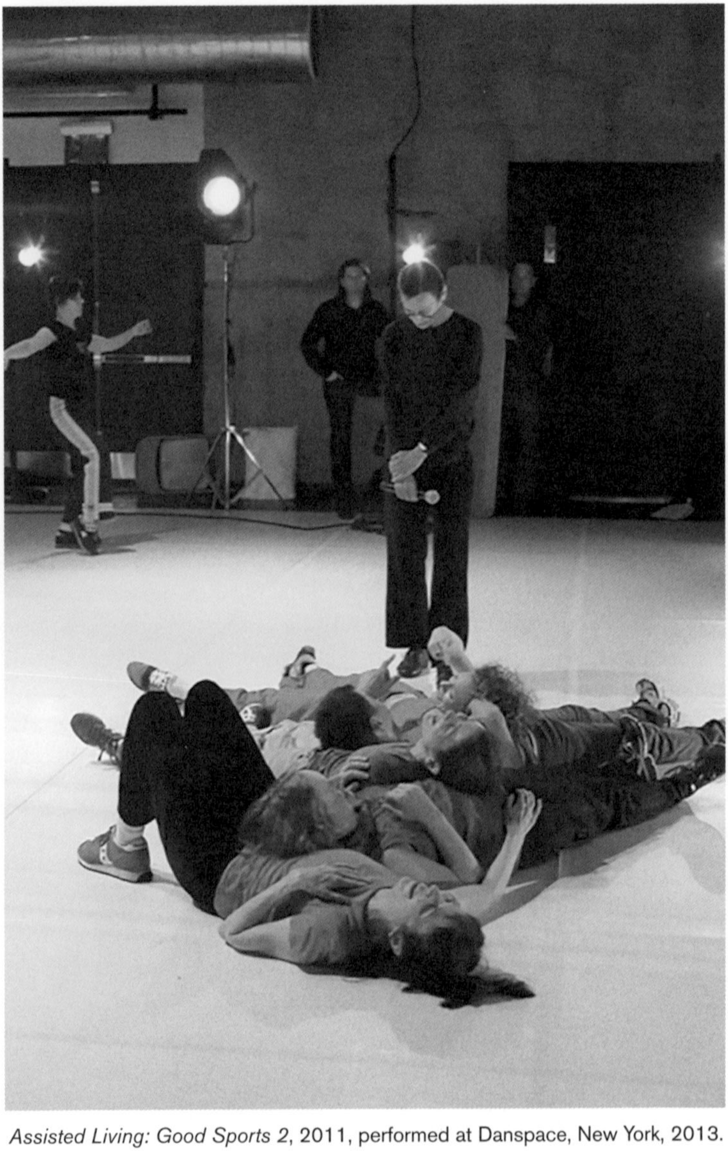

Assisted Living: Good Sports 2, 2011, performed at Danspace, New York, 2013.

performed *Trio A* that way. The flags waved around and revealed our privates. I considered it a double protest against censorship and war.

CRIMP: The flag show coincided more or less with the time that you turned from making dances to making feature films. Your first feature film, *Lives of Performers*, was released in 1972. Was it the political climate of that moment that contributed that change?

RAINER: It was the second wave of feminism. I read Kate Millett and Shulamith Firestone. I guess these writings gave me permission to investigate, in that first film, emotional life and sexual ambivalence. It wasn't so much global politics—that came later. It wasn't until my third film, *Kristina Talking Pictures*, 1976, which was about oil tankers and pollution, that I began to explore issues beyond private life.

CRIMP: Or issues that were both personal and public for you—race, breast cancer. When you became a filmmaker, your work became extremely topical. Of course, formally, your films still used the radical juxtapositions that you'd been using in your dances.

RAINER: Right. Initially, I saw an opening between avant-garde film and Hollywood "women's weepies." I had followed the "New American Cinema"—Maya Deren, Stan Brakhage, Hollis Frampton, Andy Warhol—and I saw an opening for using experimental devices in relation to a different kind of content. I didn't feel I could do that in dance. It was mainly language that would deliver this content. Film offered the possibility of using language in many different forms—voice-over, subtitles, intertitles, even newsprint pasted on my face, and eventually lip-sync.

CRIMP: I know that filmmaking was more than a full-time occupation for you, but during the time you made films, did you continue to have an interest in dance?

RAINER: Right. I continued to follow the work of my peers. I went to every Trisha Brown or David Gordon concert. But otherwise, I pretty much lost contact with dance. I was going to films. I still had images of movement, and I would pass them along to Trisha, knowing she wouldn't use them. [*Laughs.*]

CRIMP: Then in 1999, you danced a version of *Trio A* called *Trio A Pressured* at Judson, and Mikhail Baryshnikov saw you and invited you to make something for his White Oak Dance Project.

RAINER: Right. I raided my icebox to make *After Many a Summer Dies the Swan* for White Oak. Fortunately, Pat Catterson offered her services. Pat had studied with me at Connecticut College in 1969, and she's still going strong and remains devoted to my work while doing her own choreography. She knew *Trio A* and remembered other things from my past. She has a memory like a steel trap. And so I was able to make a kind of mélange using fragments from my 1960s work, together with some new speech fragments. There were six dancers, including Baryshnikov, and they passed around a microphone and recited deathbed utterances that I culled from various sources, some remarks about aging, some political stuff.

CRIMP: I guess at the time you figured *After Many a Summer Dies the Swan* would be a one-off thing rather than what it led to: a full-scale return to choreography.

RAINER: [*Laughs.*] Well, I'm still raiding it. *Swan* was followed by *Past Forward*, White Oak's Judson program. Misha continued to be interested in this period of work, and I taught *Trio A* to his company. In the meantime, I made a video using rehearsal footage from *Swan—After Many a Summer Dies the Swan: Hybrid and Rainer Variations* with Charlie Atlas. Then came the commission from Annie-B Parson for the Sourcing Stravinsky program at Dance Theater Workshop.

CRIMP: You did, in quick succession, two Stravinsky pieces, *AG Indexical, with a Little Help from H.M.*, and *RoS Indexical*. So you raided other choreographers' histories, remaking—or *revisioning*, to use your term—Balanchine's *Agon* and Nijinsky's *The Rite of Spring*.

RAINER: I was interested in those ruptures in dance history. *The Rite of Spring* is the most notorious, of course, then, in its own way, *Agon* is another, and it's one of my favorite Balanchine pieces. So, yeah, I took those on, again with Pat Catterson's help. Now I'm doing another revision, strangely enough. I teach at the University of California, Irvine, and I have eight performers, a few of them from the dance department and the rest from Studio Art.* I'm making something called *RoS Indexical Indexical*. [*Laughs.*] I'm culling from *RoS Indexical*, much of which was itself culled from Millicent Hodson's reconstruction of *The Rite of Spring*, but also again raiding that early icebox to disinter some movement games for the nondancers.

CRIMP: So you're making a new dance from *RoS Indexical*?

RAINER: It may turn out to be an interesting mess. I'll use the same soundtrack from the BBC *Riot at the Rite,* but none of the movements will be on the music. I'm doing it in reverse, beginning the dance by copying the end moves of RoS, while the music will be heard in its original form, that is, from the BBC film. Do you follow me?

CRIMP: Oh my gosh. You certainly ask a lot of your dancers. But, then, you ask a lot of yourself. That's so exciting. I hope that I get a chance to see it.

RAINER: Not many people are gonna see it. [*Laughs.*]

CRIMP: You never know, you may end up touring it.

RAINER: Ha! In a blue moon.

*Rainer taught a course called "Approaches to Performance" in the Art Department of the University of California, Irvine, from 2006 to 2013.

Challenging the Canonical:
Yvonne Rainer's *AG Indexical, with a Little Help from H.M.*
Anna P. Staniczenko

In 2006, the Dance Theater Workshop in New York City showcased new work by choreographers who had been challenged by dancer and director Annie-B Parson to "source Stravinsky." Among the most anticipated works of the evening was a new piece by Yvonne Rainer, her first in over thirty years. Rainer, one of the most "prolific and polemical" of the Judson Dance Theater choreographers in the 1960s and early '70s, had left dance in 1975 to explore filmmaking.[1] Although she had re-presented seminal earlier works like *Trio A* (1966), *AG Indexical, with a Little Help from H.M.* marked her public return to choreography.

As dance historian Sally Banes has noted, Rainer is considered the exemplar of postmodern choreography, often "to her own displeasure"; indeed, the postmodern dance movement tends to have been reduced by the general public "into a single enterprise with Rainer in the lead."[2] Grounded in her interest in task performance and everyday movement, *Trio A*, for example, violates

> nearly every canon of classic dance conventions (both ballet and modern), [bringing] classical lines and gestures into conflict with their own subversions, to create an entirely new mode of dance.[3]

It was therefore all the more surprising to see Rainer take up perhaps the most classic and famous ballet of Western history for her return to the stage. *AG Indexical, with a Little Help from H.M.* is Rainer's "re-vision" of George Balanchine's 1957 *Agon*. Rainer revised Balanchine's thirty-minute, twelve-dancer ballet for men and women into a seventeen-minute piece for four women, choosing as her dancers three veterans of the modern and postmodern dance world, Pat Catterson, Patricia Hoffbauer, and Sally Silvers, and one classically trained ballerina, Emily Coates.

If audiences expected Rainer to compose something similar to *Trio A*, they were to be disappointed. Rainer's dance responded to the expectations and standards evolving from Balanchine's *Agon* and her own *Trio A.*, challenging the canon surrounding both traditional ballet and postmodern dance.

At first glance, Balanchine in *Agon* and Rainer in *Trio A* appear to have made very different choreographic choices. Balanchine uses the body as a sculptural tool, molding his dancers into geometric shapes and patterns to fit his singular notion of beauty. With their difficult steps and complicated sequences, Balanchine's dances push technical ability and athleticism to their limits. Throughout, movement is presented to and preformed for the audience, cheeks lifted as if waiting for a kiss.

Rainer's choices are different. In *Trio A*, much of the movement is pedestrian and relies on one or two body parts per "step," and none of it requires extreme technical ability (there are no big jumps or turns, for example). Most notably, dancers in Rainer's piece never look at the audience. In refusing to do so–instead facing away or closing their eyes–the dancers acknowledge the spectators without presenting their movements directly to them.

Despite these differences, Balanchine and Rainer share qualities. Both are artists of the avant-garde. *Agon* modernized and "Americanized" ballet, shattering precedents set by previous ballets that could be called soft, even lethargic. It created a new definition of beauty, one that relied on controlled movement, abstract patterns, and an urgent dynamic. Rainer's piece, created only a few years later, was equally dramatically unconventional, but in disparate ways. Never before had movement like hers been considered dance. She choreographed steps to be as awkward as possible, added phrases that were goofy (like ear-flapping), and refused to confront her audience. Balanchine and Rainer also shared an insistence on precision. For Balanchine, it was in the form of sharp kicks, accurate turns, and detailed geometric shapes. Rainer was rigorous in her facing, focus, and placement of arms, hands, legs, and feet.

Agon and *Trio A* thus both challenged audience expectations and redefined dance aesthetics. Both are classics in Western dance history. And in *AG Indexical*, Rainer responds to the canonization of both pieces by revising *Agon* and moving away from her earlier choices in *Trio A*, even as she lifts and reshuffles sequences from both.

One of the most striking elements of *Agon* when it was first performed was the relationship of the dancers to each other. This was most notable in the pas de deux. First danced by Arthur Mitchell and Diana Adams, the piece shattered formal balletic partnering structure:

> Turning *pas de deux* conventions upside down, the boy with bold grace supports the girl and pivots her on *pointe*, lying on his back on the floor. At one moment classic movements turned inside out become intimate gestures. At another a pose forced way beyond its classic ending reveals

> a novel harmony. At still another, the mutual first tremor of an uncertain supported balance is so isolated musically it becomes a dance movement. So does the dangerous scoop out of balance and back into balance of the girl supported on *pointe*. The dance flows through stops, through scooping changes on pace, through differences of pace between the partners as they hold each other by the hand.[4]

Besides the unexpected physical manipulation of the dancers, audiences would have been unable to ignore the fact that Mitchell was black and Adams white. Balanchine did not intend for this to be a political statement, although in the shadow of the civil rights movement it was inevitably so. More important to Balanchine was the way in which their difference in skin tone introduced a color structure into the choreographic one.[5] As another dancer commented, "It was really awesome to see a black hand touch a white skin."[6]

Throughout *Agon*, dancers were brought together in an innovative fashion. The word "agon" is Greek for "contest," and although a program note asks audience members to overlook the etymology, it was difficult not to notice the dancers' "urgent necessity" and athleticism.[7] As one critic describes it: "The man is no longer the faintly creaky aristocrat, but a bold young male with two slinky and competitive women on his hands."[8] Later in the piece, two men "ball their hands into fists and thrust out their chests as they jump in adversarial poses."[9] Balanchine thus created a dynamic between the dancers that was essential to the ballet's impulse and spawned its innovative movement.

Rainer chooses to place these distinguished and highly celebrated movements within a different context, one that transforms the relationship of the dancers to each other. Rather than adversaries, the dancers in *AG Indexical* are comrades. They are, as Deborah Jowitt writes, "in this together and let you know it, sitting on an incongruous flowered ottoman to watch one another."[10] Three clap along like castanets to another's solo. As one balances on rélévé, two hold her hands and right her as she sways off balance. When they switch hands, they do so urgently, knowing that without their support she may topple.

Balanchine's *pas de deux* is masterfully redesigned as a quartet to highlight the group-effort manipulation of a ballerina. First, the famous attitude pose appears with Coates wrapped around and supported by the other three. Catterson, Silvers, and Hoffbauer then proceed to gently move Coates into the familiar positions of Diana Adams in *Agon*. Together, they hold her hand, move her feet, pivot her around, and guide each other using traffic-control signals. The celebrated shapes in which Mitchell and Adams were intertwined are brought into relief by this revising of the movement impulse, and, in their new context, they are as fresh and innovative as they were in 1957.

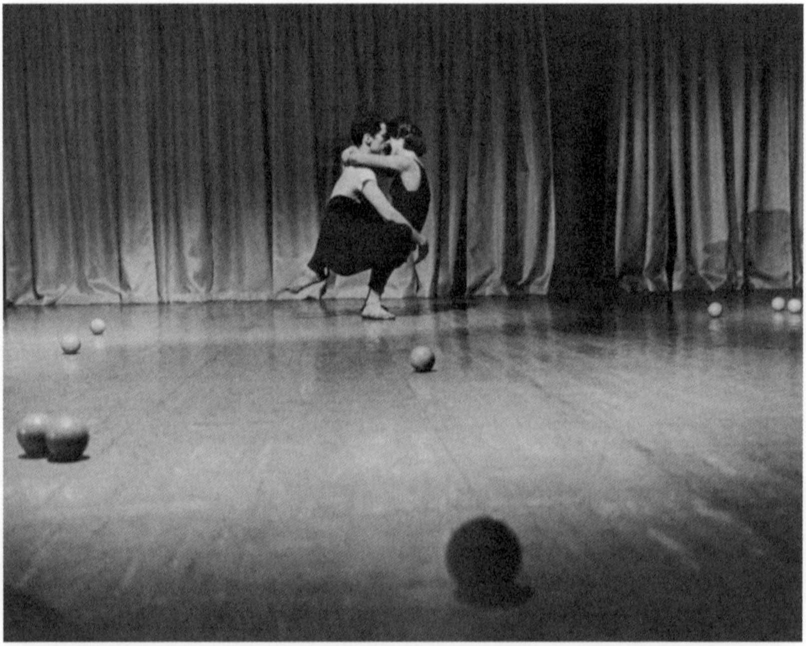

William Davis and Yvonne Rainer in "Love," part of *Terrain*, 1963. Performed at Judson Memorial Church, New York, 1963. © 2020 Hottelet / Giese / Licensed by Artists Rights Society (ARS), New York.

While Balanchine regarded the body as a raw material to be manipulated, Rainer approaches the body as a machine in need of repair. In an interview with Clarinda Mac Low, she explains that her version of the *pas de deux* treats the "ballerina as a machine of some kind that has broken down and has to be carefully handled."[11] It is a dramatically different conception of how the dancers relate to one other, and it boldly reconfigures what many dance historians consider the crucial element of *Agon*. But the way in which the four dancers work together is also distinct from Rainer's own *Trio A*, in which each performs to his or her own tempo while seemingly ignoring the others (particularly evident in *Trio A*'s "facing" variation, in which someone attempts, usually in vain, to keep their face in front of the dancer's at all times). In *AG Indexical*, Rainer thus shifts from her previous inclinations and exposes the audience to a different choreographic intent regarding dancer-to-dancer relationships.

AG Indexical, with a Little Help from H.M. brilliantly manages to mesh Rainer's pedestrian movement with Balanchine's technical sequences—and it does so without becoming a parody. One way Rainer achieves this is by casting dancers with different levels of training. This choice articulates her intention to juxtapose movement on different bodies and sets up a dynamic relationship to formal technique.[12] With only ballerinas, this piece might appear to plagiarize Balanchine's work; with four completely untrained dancers, it might seem instead a parody.

Rainer sets Balanchine's movement phrases on her four dancers at the very beginning, with a few edits and additions. As they start to dance, different technical abilities become immediately apparent. Coates is obviously a highly trained ballerina. Two dancers appear to have some training; one seems to have barely any. The varying technical abilities mean that while Coates's performance is close to the original, other movements barely resemble the original ballet. Furthermore, the women are of different ages and have different body types. As a result, the movement reveals itself differently on each.

Rainer's earlier approach to choreography can be most clearly located in "Double and Triple Pas-de-Quatre (Taisha's solo)," danced by Hoffbauer and Coates. Performed alongside a monitor showing *Agon*, Hoffbauer's solo consists of rapid, precise foot movements made in place with slowly changing arms. The arm movements vary in form, sometimes referencing ballet, and frequently corresponding with the movement on the monitor in terms of tension and speed. Hoffbauer then slows into a sequence with extended arms and legs that does not obviously reference Balanchine's work. Meanwhile, Coates proceeds to run around stage, turning only in right angles, swinging her arms as she changes direction suddenly and shuffling slightly in pointe shoes. This section of the piece would be the favorite for fans of Rainer's early work, as it rebuffs the highly technical choreography on the video monitor.

But Rainer shifts her approach to technique two sections later, when Pat Catterson performs "Bransle Gay" step by step, and with visible pride at her ability to execute the steps cleanly, even though she is not a ballerina. In the next section, Sally Silvers attempts to follow along with a piece she has only seen once before using the video monitor. As she bumbles through, the bizarreness of Balanchine's choreography becomes especially apparent, and we are reminded how unnatural ballet steps can be. Immediately following, Catterson and Coates dance excerpts from *Trio A*, with Balanchine movements spliced in.

Until now, Coates has been dancing in pointe shoes. Just as in Silvers's solo, the effect is to accentuate the bizarre deformations of the body in ballet, as a normal body performs Balanchine ballet steps and a ballet body—pointe shoes are key in making it a "true" ballet body—performs pedestrian movements. The choice to work within and around a formal technique like Balanchine's is perhaps the most dramatic aspect of Rainer's response to the canon surrounding *Agon* and her past work. Putting non-ballerinas in the piece is a vehement claim that their dancing is just as beautiful as that of New York City Ballet dancers. This clearly challenges the standards of *Agon* and the requirements of highly trained professionals for Balanchine's choreography. Simply by placing Coates in pointe shoes, Rainer has already taken a huge step away from *Trio A* and her previous beliefs about classical dance conventions. For those expecting to see a dance that reprised her past work, *AG Indexical* was too dance-oriented, a betrayal of the manifestos on which they had based their concepts of postmodern dance. Some were disappointed, even angry. Whether or not Rainer intended for such an intense reaction to *AG Indexical*, it certainly made clear her wishes away from *Trio A*. This does not imply forgetting it–she continues to teach and work with the piece (it was even excerpted in *AG Indexical*). But thirty years later, Rainer has had enough time to rework some of her creative choices and to push them into a new analytic realm.

The last choreographic choice in *AG Indexical, with a Little Help from H.M.* that I will discuss here is Rainer's decision about the music. In keeping with the spirit of the "Sourcing Stravinsky" program, Rainer kept the Stravinsky score in the first parts of the dance. A twelve-tone piece with a serial structure, Stravinsky's music is so complicated that musicians today are unable to deconstruct it completely.[13] It was unlike anything the composer had previous written; in fact, he was worried it would not be well received. Indeed, the ballet was as unconventional as it was in part because of its musical score. Balanchine "understood that *Agon*'s 'differentness' demanded a new approach–an approach, he wrote, that would produce a 'visual equivalent which is a complement; not an illustration'"; that is to say, Stravinsky's orchestration of the piece was crucial to Balanchine's choreographic concept.[14]

Unlike Balanchine, who studied the score carefully in order to fit the dance to its substructure, Rainer describes herself as "unmusical."[15] She did not have a full grasp of the Stravinsky score while creating *AG Indexical*. But despite this, she resets certain phrases of *Agon* and her own *Trio A* (as well as *Three Satie Spoons*) so that they go very well with the complicated score. When asked how she succeeded in such a difficult task, one that departed significantly from the silence of *Trio A*, Rainer simply stated that she "kept seeing those steps to the music in her head."[16]

But Rainer didn't just use the Stravinsky score; she also restaged the first quartet to Henry Mancini's *Pink Panther* theme. Her choice to reset her variation on the first quartet to the familiar bars by Mancini is a not-so-subtle reaction to the canonization of Stravinsky's score. But despite this cheeky irreverence, Rainer is in no way disrespectful of the celebrated composer and choreographer pair. She could have been, had she wanted to–perhaps by setting the piece to an explicit pop song. Instead, Rainer acknowledges the composer's-and-choreographer's jazz influences by choosing the Mancini piece–and not just any jazz piece, but one that is itself considered canonical. It is clear, however, that setting these steps to the *Pink Panther* theme brings a new dimension to the original choreography. It may be shocking to some that after decades of analysis of *Agon*, the most refreshing new dimension of the piece is revealed by using new music. It seems appropriate, however, that it would be a postmodernist – like Rainer – who would realize this potential and expose it.

In many ways, then, *AG Indexical, with a Little Help from H.M.* aligns itself theoretically with Rainer's previous work in the avant-garde. It is precise in design, and places familiar and famous steps in a fresh analytical context. It redesigns dancer-to-dancer relationships and reworks Rainer's previous reactions to formal technique. It acknowledges the brilliance of the composer and choreographer's work respectfully but also irreverently as it restages the piece to Mancini's music. As Rainer said in the interview with Mac Low, "There's a way in which my *AG Indexical* is a pedagogical enterprise. It's informative and analytical." And while many fans of the postmodern movement may find its performance quality to be antithetical to her classic work, they must realize that Rainer's beliefs about breaking rules would of course extend to her own. *AG Indexical, with a Little Help from H.M.* is a response to the canonizing of *Agon* and *Trio A*, and a bold challenge to audience expectations about both classical and postmodern dance aesthetics.

1. Sally Banes, *Terpsichore in Sneakers* (Middletown: Wesleyan University Press, 1987), p. 41.
2. Ibid., p. 42.
3. Ibid., p. 44.
4. Edwin Denby, "Three Sides to *Agon*," in *Dance Writings and Poetry* (New Haven: Yale University Press, 1998), p. 268.
5. Ibid.
6. Quoted in Charles Joseph, *Stravinsky and Balanchine: A Journey of Invention* (New Haven: Yale University Press, 2002), p. 257.
7. Ibid. p. 263.
8. Quoted in ibid., p. 266.
9. Quoted in ibid., p. 269.
10. Deborah Jowitt, "Wake up, Igor," *The Village Voice*, April 24, 2006.
11. Clarinda Mac Low, "Yvonne Rainer in Conversation with Clarinda Mac Low," *Movement Research*, April 3, 2006, https://movementresearch.org/publications/critical-correspondenceyvonne-rainer-in-conversation-with-clarinda-mac-low.
12. The term "formal technique" refers to Balanchine's ballet technique but also to general technical ability, which Rainer vehemently combined with pedestrian movement, both so essential to her early choreography.
13. Joseph, *Stravinsky and Balanchine*, p. 260.
14. Ibid., p. 259.
15. Mac Low, "Yvonne Rainer in Conversation."
16. Ibid.

Epilogue: Program Notes to *Parts of Some Sextets*

Statement by Yvonne Rainer:

Parts of Some Sextets is both a reconstruction and reconfiguration of a dance of the same name, initially performed by ten people with twelve mattresses and presented at the Wadsworth Atheneum of Music and Art and Judson Memorial Church in 1965. The original ten performers were Lucinda Childs, Judith Dunn, Sally Gross, Deborah Hay, Tony Holder, Robert Morris, Steve Paxton, Yvonne Rainer, Robert Rauschenberg, and Joseph Schlichter.

At that time, after we had learned all of the dance moves and tasks, I created an elaborate score, then joined my fellow performers to begin building the dance. The process required that we continually consult two sheets of graph paper pinned to a wall of my studio that contained a timeline plus words and initials assigning specific movements and tasks to individual performers. We rehearsed three or four times a week for at least eight weeks. I rarely, if at all, stood apart from the goings-on as a detached observer.

During the 2019 rehearsals, now in the role of director rather than performer, I found myself once again acknowledging the influence of Alain Robbe-Grillet's *For a New Novel*, a tract that I and many of my contemporaries were absorbing in the early 1960s. Back then, its critique of nineteenth-century Romanticism and narrative conventions was launching a number of artists' ships, *Parts of Some Sextets* among them.

The present rendition owes much to the initiative and persuasiveness of Emily Coates. Many months prior to our first rehearsal, she had traveled to the Getty Research Institute in Los Angeles to dig out traces of *PoSS* in my archive. Despite the fact that she was not yet born in 1965, she continually reassured me that the entire enterprise would require less time to complete than previously and would be well worth the effort. Her intuitions proved to be correct. It took ten days in June to sketch out the dance and ten more to polish it in August. Without Emily's initial confidence, I would never have touched "the mattress monster!" And without her unflagging optimism and assistance, it might never have seen the light of the present day.

I must also applaud the current eleven performers for their good will and patience as they hung in with the arduous process and my occasional befuddlement, as there was no film or video documentation of the earlier version to guide us, only Peter Moore's photographs, a brief essay by me, and the first half of the original score (the other half long vanished). The performers not only learned all the moves (some of which needed re-invention), they had to listen for word phrases in the Bentley texts that in my voice-over reading signaled total or partial changes in the field of vision every thirty seconds! I am filled with gratitude and admiration for all who have been involved in this project.

Statement by Emily Coates:

When I arrived at the Rauschenberg Foundation on August 29, 2019, I discovered that Yvonne had beaten me by fifteen minutes. I found her sitting tall at a computer in their library, her ears encased in large black headphones, her glasses glowing from the light of the screen. She was listening intently to her thirty-year-old self reading the Bentley text that accompanies *Parts of Some Sextets*. She had recorded the voice-over in her living room on East 25th Street on a Wollensak reel-to-reel tape recorder around 1:00 a.m. in January 1965. Traffic hums in the background. Until that day in August, we thought the recording had vanished.

I had hoped to catch her first reaction, a moment of reckoning with her past, but she had already been listening for a while. "Yeah, that seems to be it," she simply said. Behind her on a long table lay the original quarter-inch reel-to-reel. On the front of the plastic case, Rauschenberg had written on a piece of masking tape, now brown with age, "CH 1: RAINER: PARTS FROM SOME SEXTETS." He then stored the recording in his basement for decades. The tape's survival felt like a small miracle.

Parts of Some Sextets is a missing puzzle piece in Yvonne's oeuvre: Its excesses—ten performers, twelve mattresses, her voice-over reading from a minister's late-eighteenth-century diaries, a systematic score in which she plays with disjunctive continuity and duration—predate by one year the economy and flow of her seminal dance *Trio A*. And yet only a handful of people living today saw *PoSS* when it was performed in March 1965—and never again.

The research for this revival began with a trip I took in August 2018 to the Getty Research Institute, where Yvonne's papers are housed, and culminated in our visit to the Rauschenberg Foundation one year later. My role in this process has been that of instigator, information sleuth, memory jogger, pep talker, co-puzzle decipherer, kinesthetic conjurer, and overall Rainer tracker.

One thing is clear: Rainer is difficult to track. If she headed into this process with some trepidation, she flew through it as we went along, with each archival detail put before her getting whisked up and either definitively established or speedily reinvented. Throughout this work, Yvonne encountered her youthful self almost as if she were another artist and this was a new dance. The scene at the foundation suggests a provocative revival: The passing of time changes the technology and the materials of art-making no less than the perspective of the artist as she ages. But the art endures. As Yvonne wrote to me recently, “Life is short. Art is forever.” Reborn from 1965 documentation, this evening’s dance begins in February 1786 and comes to a second fruition 233 years later in November 2019. Enjoy. Ovidigendae ad et harum eosapel iquosap erumqui quatem nimusamus adi optate debis niti

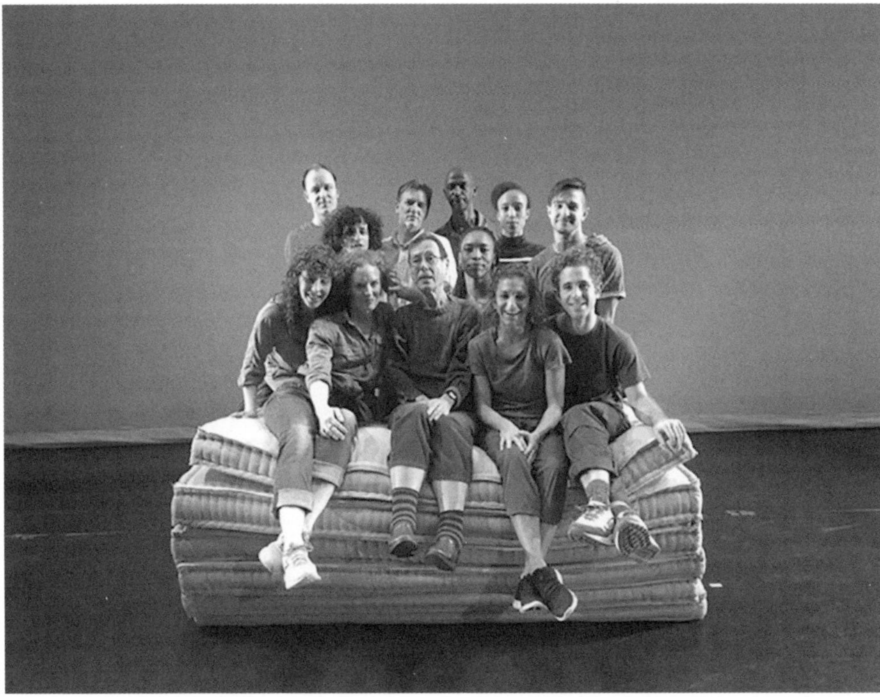

Liz Magic Laser, Nick Mauss, Rachel Bernsen, Emily Coates, Jon Kinzel, Yvonne Rainer, David Thomson, Shayla-Vie Jenkins, Brittany Engel-Adams, Mary Kate Sheehan, Timothy Ward, and Patrick Gallagher, rehearsal image of *Parts of Some Sextets*, 2019. Performed as part of Performa 19 at Gelsey Kirkland Arts Center, Brooklyn, 2019.

Choreography, 1961–2020

<u>1961–62</u>
Three Satie Spoons
Satie for Two
Grass
Three Seascapes
Dance for 3 People and 6 Arms
Ordinary Dance

<u>1963–65</u>
We Shall Run
Terrain
Room Service
At My Body's House
Dialogues
Some Thoughts on Improvisation
Part of a Sextet
Incidents
Parts of Some Sextets

<u>1966–68</u>
The Mind Is a Muscle, Part 1 (Trio A)
Carriage Discreteness
The Mind Is a Muscle (final version)
Performance Demonstration
Body and Snot
Northeast Passing

<u>1969–71</u>
Chair-Pillow
Rose Fractions
Performance Fractions for the West Coast
Connecticut Composite
Continuous Project-Altered Daily
WAR
Trio A With Flags
Grand Union Dreams
Numerous Frames

1972–73
In the College
Performance
This Is the Story of a Woman Who . . .
Kristina (for a . . . Novella)

1999–2000
Trio A Pressured
After Many a Summer Dies the Swan

2006–2012
AG Indexical, with a little help from H.M.
RoS Indexical
Spiraling Down
Trio A in Ten Easy Lessons
Good Sports
Trio A: Geriatric With Talking
Assisted Living: Good Sports 2
Lamentable

2013–2020
Assisted Living: Do you have any money?
The Concept of Dust, or How do you look when there's nothing left to move?
The Concept of Dust: Continuous Project-Altered Annually Again? What now?
Remembering and Dismembering Trio A with Peter Schjeldahl's "77 Sunset Me"

Acknowledgments

"Pedagogical Vaudeville 3" was first published in *PAJ, a Journal of Performance Art* 23, no. 1 (January 2001), pp. 48–61. It is reprinted here with permission of MIT Press.

Rainer's interview with Douglas Crimp was first published as "Dance Mom: An Interview" in *Interview*, December 2012. Parts of the conversation that were not included in the final online version published in 2012 have been reinstated here with permission by Rainer and the Estate of Douglas Crimp.

"Challenging the Canonical: Yvonne Rainer's *AG Indexical with a Little Help from H.M.*" by Anna Goddu Staniczenko was written for Emily Coates's "Dance Theater" course at Yale University in 2006. Staniczenko is currently a resident in OB/GYN at Columbia Medical Center – New York Presbyterian Hospital. We are grateful for her permission to include the essay in this volume.

Yvonne Rainer's and Emily Coates's statements in the Epilogue were included in the program notes for the performance of *Parts of Some Sextets*, presented November 15–17 at the Gelsey Kirkland Arts Center as part of Performa 19.

no place press catalogue:

Jordan Kantor: Selected Exhibitions 2006–2016
Conversation with Yve-Alain Bois

Bill Berkson, *A Frank O'Hara Notebook*
Contributions by Ron Padgett and Constance M. Lewallen

Pamela M. Lee, *The Glen Park Library: A Fairy Tale of Disruption*
Foreword by Michelle Kuo

Anne Walsh, *Hello Leonora, Soy Anne Walsh*
Contributions by Dodie Bellamy, Julia Bryan-Wilson, and Claudia La Rocco

Amy Franceschini and Michael Swaine, Futurefarmers, *For Want of a Nail*
Contributions by Peter Galison, Patrick Kiley, Lucy Lippard, Megan Prelinger and Rick Prelinger, and Anne Walsh

Yvonne Rainer, *Revisions, Essays by Apollo Musagète, Yvonne Rainer, and Others*
Contributions by Gregg Bordowitz, Emily Coates, Douglas Crimp, and Anna Staniczenko